SUPREME

WATCH 2013

*Highlights of the 2010, 2011, and 2012 Terms
and Preview of the 2013 Term*

DAVID M. O'BRIEN
UNIVERSITY OF VIRGINIA

W • W • **NORTON & COMPANY** • NEW YORK • LONDON

W. W. Norton & Company has been independent since its founding in 1923, when William Warder Norton and Mary D. Herter Norton first published lectures delivered at the People's Institute, the adult education division of New York City's Cooper Union. The firm soon expanded its program beyond the Institute, publishing books by celebrated academics from America and abroad. By mid-century, the two major pillars of Norton's publishing program—trade books and college texts—were firmly established. In the 1950s, the Norton family transferred control of the company to its employees, and today—with a staff of four hundred and a comparable number of trade, college, and professional titles published each year—W. W. Norton & Company stands as the largest and oldest publishing house owned wholly by its employees.

Editor: Lisa Camner McKay
Assistant Editor: Sarah Wolf
Marketing Manager: Erin Brown
Composition by Cathy Lombardi
Manufacturing by Sterling Pierce
Managing Editor, College: Marian Johnson
Production Manager: Vanessa Nuttry

ISBN: 978-0-393-93650-6

W. W. Norton & Company, Inc., 500 Fifth Avenue, New York, NY 10110-0017
www.wwnorton.com

W. W. Norton & Company Ltd., Castle House, 75/76 Wells Street,
London W1T 3QT

1 2 3 4 5 6 7 8 9 0

CONTENTS

PREFACE   ix

VOLUME ONE

CHAPTER 2 ▪ *Law and Politics in the Supreme Court: Jurisdiction and Decision-Making Process*   1

◻ INSIDE THE COURT: The Court's Disposition of Appeals in the 2012–2013 Term   2

A. JURISDICTION AND JUSTICIABLE CONTROVERSIES   3
[*M. B. Z. v. Clinton*]   3
[*Camreta v. Greene*]   3
Hollingsworth v. Perry   4
◻ THE DEVELOPMENT OF LAW: Class-Action Suits   7
[*Bond v. United States*]   8
[*Clapper v. Amnesty International*]   9
Arizona Christian School Tuition Organization v. Winn   9

B. THE COURT'S DOCKET AND SCREENING CASES   13
◻ INSIDE THE COURT: The Business of the Supreme Court in the 2012–2013 Term   13

H. OPINION DAYS AND COMMUNICATING DECISIONS   14
◻ INSIDE THE COURT: Opinion Writing during the 2012–2013 Term   14

CHAPTER 4 ▪ *The President as Chief Executive in Domestic Affairs*   15

[*City of Arlington v. FCC*]   15
B. APPOINTMENT AND REMOVAL POWERS   16
[*National Labor Relations Board v. Canning*]   16

CHAPTER 6 ■ *Congress: Legislative, Taxing, and Spending Powers* 17

C. From the New Deal Crisis to the Administrative State 17

[*National Federation of Independent Business v. Sebelius*] 17

D. Taxing and Spending Powers 18

National Federation of Independent Business v. Sebelius 18

CHAPTER 7 ■ *The States and American Federalism* 33

A. States' Power over Commerce and Regulation 33

□ THE DEVELOPMENT OF LAW: Other Rulings on State Regulatory Powers in Alleged Conflict with Federal Legislation 33

B. The Tenth and Eleventh Amendments and the States 35

[*Arizona v. United States*] 35

□ THE DEVELOPMENT OF LAW: Other Recent Rulings on the Tenth Amendment 35

□ THE DEVELOPMENT OF LAW: Other Recent Rulings on the Eleventh Amendment 36

CHAPTER 8 ■ *Representative Government, Voting Rights, and Electoral Politics* 37

A. Representative Government and the Franchise 37

□ THE DEVELOPMENT OF LAW: Other Rulings Interpreting the Voting Rights Act 37

B. Voting Rights and the Reapportionment Revolution 38

[*Tennant v. Jefferson County Commission*] 38

[*Shelby County, Alabama v. Holder*] 38

C. Campaigns and Elections 39

[*American Tradition Partnership v. Bullock*] 40

[*Arizona v. Inter Tribal Council of Arizona*]   40

Arizona Free Enterprise Club's Freedom Club PAC v. Bennett   40

□ THE DEVELOPMENT OF LAW: Other Rulings on Campaigns and Elections   48

CHAPTER 9 ■ *Economic Rights and American Capitalism*   49

□ THE DEVELOPMENT OF LAW: Other Rulings on the Takings Clause   49

VOLUME TWO

CHAPTER 4 ■ *The Nationalization of the Bill of Rights*   53

B. THE RISE AND (PARTIAL) RETREAT OF THE "DUE PROCESS REVOLUTION"   53

□ THE DEVELOPMENT OF LAW: Other Recent Rulings on Substantive and Procedural Due Process   53

CHAPTER 5 ■ *Freedom of Expression and Association*   55

[*Golan v. Holder*]   55

A. JUDICIAL APPROACHES TO THE FIRST AMENDMENT   56
(2) JUDICIAL LINE DRAWING: AD HOC AND DEFINITIONAL BALANCING   56

[*United States v. Alvarez*]   56

[*Agency for International Development v. Alliance for Open Society International, Inc.*]   56

Brown v. Entertainment Merchants Association   57

D. COMMERCIAL SPEECH   63

□ THE DEVELOPMENT OF LAW: Other Important Rulings on Commercial Speech and the First Amendment   63

F. REGULATING THE BROADCAST AND CABLE MEDIA, AND THE INTERNET   64

[*FCC v. Fox Television Stations, Inc.*]   64

H. SYMBOLIC SPEECH AND SPEECH-PLUS-CONDUCT   64
   (2) SPEECH-PLUS-CONDUCT   64
   Snyder v. Phelps   65

CHAPTER 6 ■ *Freedom from and of Religion*   68

A. THE (DIS)ESTABLISHMENT OF RELIGION   68
   [*Hosanna-Tabor Evangelical Lutheran Church and School v. Equal
   Employment Opportunity Commission*]   68
   [*Town of Greece v. Galloway*]   69

CHAPTER 7 ■ *The Fourth Amendment Guarantee against
Unreasonable Searches and Seizures*   70

   [*Maryland v. King*]   70

A. REQUIREMENTS FOR A WARRANT AND REASONABLE
SEARCHES AND SEIZURES   71
   United States v. Jones   72
   Florida v. Jardines   80

B. EXCEPTIONS TO THE FOURTH AMENDMENT WARRANT
REQUIREMENT   86
   [*Florence v. Board of Chosen Freeholders*]   86
   [*Bailey v. United States*]   87
   [*Missouri v. McNeely*]   87
   Kentucky v. King   88

C. THE SPECIAL PROBLEMS OF AUTOMOBILES IN A
MOBILE SOCIETY   91
   [*Florida v. Harris*]   91

F. THE EXCLUSIONARY RULE   92
   Davis v. United States   92

CHAPTER 8 ■ *The Fifth Amendment Guarantee against
Self-Accusation*   97

A. COERCED CONFESSIONS AND POLICE
INTERROGATIONS   97

[*Howes v. Fields*]   97

[*Salinas v. Texas*]   98

J. D. B. v. North Carolina   98

□ THE DEVELOPMENT OF LAW: Other Court Rulings on Coerced
Confessions and Limiting *Miranda*   101

C. REAL VERSUS TESTIMONIAL EVIDENCE   102

[*Missouri v. McNeely*] (reprise)   102

□ THE DEVELOPMENT OF LAW: Rulings on Real versus Testimonial
Evidence   103

CHAPTER 9 ■ *The Right to Counsel and Other Procedural Guarantees*   104

A. THE RIGHT TO COUNSEL   104

□ THE DEVELOPMENT OF LAW: Rulings Extending the Right
to Counsel throughout the Criminal Justice System   104

B. PLEA BARGAINING AND THE RIGHT TO EFFECTIVE
COUNSEL   104

[*Lafler v. Cooper*]   105

Missouri v. Frye   105

D. THE RIGHT TO AN IMPARTIAL JURY TRIAL   110

[*Southern Union Company v. United States*]   110

[*Alleyne v. United States*]   110

F. THE RIGHT TO BE INFORMED OF CHARGES AND TO
CONFRONT ACCUSERS   110

[*Michigan v. Bryant*]   111

[*Bullcoming v. New Mexico*]   111

[*Williams v. Illinois*]   111

G. THE GUARANTEE AGAINST DOUBLE JEOPARDY   112

[*Blueford v. Arkansas*]   112

[*Evans v. Michigan*]   113

CHAPTER 10 ■ *Cruel and Unusual Punishment*   114

[*Brown v. Plata*]   114

[*Miller v. Alabama*]   115

CHAPTER 11 ▪ The Right of Privacy 116

A. PRIVACY AND REPRODUCTIVE FREEDOM 116
[*Cline v. Oklahoma Coalition for Reproductive Justice*] 116

CHAPTER 12 ▪ The Equal Protection of the Laws 117

[*Armour v. City of Indianapolis*] 117
C. AFFIRMATIVE ACTION AND REVERSE
DISCRIMINATION 118
[*Fisher v. University of Texas at Austin*] 118
[*Schuette v. Coalition to Defend Affirmative Action*] 118

D. NONRACIAL CLASSIFICATIONS AND THE EQUAL
PROTECTION OF THE LAWS 119
(2) DISCRIMINATION AGAINST GAYS AND LESBIANS 119
[*Hollingsworth v. Perry* (reprise)] 119
United States v. Windsor 120

INDEX OF CASES 129

PREFACE

Supreme Court Watch 2013 examines the changes and decisions made during the Supreme Court's 2010, 2011, and 2012 terms. In addition to highlighting the major constitutional rulings in excerpts from leading cases, section-by-section introductions discuss other important decisions and analyze recent developments in various areas of constitutional law. The important cases that the Court has granted review and will decide in its 2013–2014 term are also previewed. To offer even more information in an efficient format, special boxes titled "The Development of Law" and "Inside the Court" are also included.

The favorable reception of previous editions of the *Watch* has been gratifying, and I hope that this twenty-third edition will further contribute to students' understanding of constitutional law, politics, and history, as well as to their appreciation for how the politics of constitutional interpretation turns on differing interpretations of constitutional politics and the role of the Supreme Court. I am most grateful to Sarah Wolf for doing an expeditious job in producing this edition.

D.M.O.
July 1, 2013

SUPREME COURT WATCH 2013
VOLUME ONE

2

LAW AND POLITICS IN THE SUPREME COURT: JURISDICTION AND DECISION-MAKING PROCESS

The October 2012 term marked Chief Justice Roberts's eighth term on the high bench. During his terms, the Court had an annual average of 8,547 cases on its docket (ranging from 8,966 to 10,256 cases). The Court also continued the trend of granting oral arguments and plenary consideration to less than 1 percent of the cases on its docket. The Roberts Court heard on average only 81 cases per term, or less than half of what the Court heard 30 years ago when the entire docket was significantly smaller. As in the past, as indicated in the table below, the Court tended to grant cases in order to reverse the lower courts' rulings and to decide more statutory interpretation cases and those involving jurisdiction, practice, and procedure.

■ Inside the Court

The Court's Disposition of Appeals in the 2012–2013 Term

	AFFIRMED	REVERSED OR VACATED
First Circuit	1	1
Second Circuit	4	7
Third Circuit	1	4
Fourth Circuit	3	3
Fifth Circuit		6
Sixth Circuit		1
Seventh Circuit	2	2
Eighth Circuit		1
Ninth Circuit	3	12
Tenth Circuit	1	1
Eleventh Circuit		6
Federal Circuit	2	2
District of Columbia Circuit		3
Other Federal Courts		2
State Courts and Other	4	7
*Totals:	21	58

*Excludes cases decided on original jurisdiction or dismissed for lack of jurisdiction or dismissed as moot or improvidently granted and remanded.

A | *Jurisdiction and Justiciable Controversies*

In its 2011–2012 term the Roberts Court evaded deciding whether Congress has the authority to dictate how the executive branch issues birth certificates for U.S. citizens born abroad. It did so in holding that the lower courts erred in ruling that the controversy presented a non-justiciable "political question" and remanded the case for consideration of the constitutionality of the statute in question. At issue in *M. B. Z. v. Clinton*, 132 S.Ct. 1421 (2012) is the validity of a 10-year-old law (Section 214(d) of Public Law 107-228) in which Congress aimed to acknowledge Jerusalem as the capital of Israel, even though the U.S. government does not recognize it as part of Israel. After State Department officials refused to fill out a report on the foreign birth of a boy—Menachem Binyamin Zivotofsky (M. B. Z.)—born in 2002 in a Jerusalem hospital to show that his birthplace was "Israel," his parents sued, seeking to enforce the 2002 law that directed the State Department to do just that, when asked to do so by the parents. A federal district court judge and the Court of Appeals for the District of Columbia Circuit refused to decide the case and held that the controversy presented a "political question" that the courts had no authority to decide.

The Roberts Court in its 2010, 2011, and 2012 terms also reinforced its interest in enforcing threshold rules, such as mootness and ripeness (see Vol. 1 or 2, Ch. 2), and thereby avoiding the questions presented in *Camreta v. Greene*, 131 S.Ct. 1465 (2011). There, Justice Kagan held that a suit against a social worker and a sheriff who allegedly violated the Fourth Amendment rights of a nine-year-old student by questioning her without a warrant about possible sexual abuse was moot because she was now almost 18 years old and had moved from California, where the incident occurred, to Florida. Justices Kennedy and Thomas dissented.

Notably, in *Hollingsworth v. Perry* (excerpted below) a bare majority denied standing to sue to enforce California's Proposition 8, a constitutional amendment banning same-sex marriages.

Hollingsworth v. Perry
133 S.Ct. 2652 (2013)

In 2008, California voters approved a state constitutional amendment, so-called Proposition 8, barring same-sex marriages, in response to a state supreme court ruling permitting same-sex marriages. A federal district court declared Proposition 8 unconstitutional, and that decision was affirmed by the U.S. Court of Appeals for the Ninth Circuit. Because state officials refused to defend Proposition 8, supporters sought standing in appealing the lower court's ruling. The Supreme Court granted review but denied standing because supporters of Proposition 8 failed to show a "personal stake" in the enforcement of the law and a particularized interest sufficient to meet the "case or controversy" requirements of Article III of the Constitution. As a result the courts' decisions remain enact. Chief Justice Roberts delivered the opinion of the Court. Justice Kennedy filed a dissenting opinion, which was joined by Justices Thomas, Alito, and Sotomayor.

□ *CHIEF JUSTICE ROBERTS delivered the opinion of the Court.*

The public is currently engaged in an active political debate over whether same-sex couples should be allowed to marry. That question has also given rise to litigation. In this case, petitioners, who oppose same-sex marriage, ask us to decide whether the Equal Protection Clause "prohibits the State of California from defining marriage as the union of a man and a woman." Respondents, same-sex couples who wish to marry, view the issue in somewhat different terms: For them, it is whether California—"having previously recognized the right of same-sex couples to marry—" may reverse that decision through a referendum. Federal courts have authority under the Constitution to answer such questions only if necessary to do so in the course of deciding an actual "case" or "controversy." As used in the Constitution, those words do not include every sort of dispute, but only those "historically viewed as capable of resolution through the judicial process." *Flast v. Cohen*, 392 U. S. 83 (1968). This is an essential limit on our power: It ensures that we act as judges, and do not engage in policymaking properly left to elected representatives.

For there to be such a case or controversy, it is not enough that the party invoking the power of the court have a keen interest in the issue. That party must also have "standing," which requires, among other things, that it have suffered a concrete and particularized injury. Because we find that petitioners do not have standing, we have no authority to decide this case on the merits, and neither did the Ninth Circuit. . . .

Article III of the Constitution confines the judicial power of federal courts to deciding actual "Cases" or "Controversies." One essential aspect of this requirement is that any person invoking the power of a federal court must demonstrate standing to do so. This requires the litigant to prove that he has suffered a concrete and particularized injury that is fairly traceable to the challenged conduct, and is likely to be redressed by a favorable judicial decision. *Lujan v. Defenders of Wildlife*, 504 U.S. 555 (1992). In other words, for a federal court to have authority under the Constitution to settle a dispute, the party before it must seek a remedy for a personal and tangible harm. . . .

Most standing cases consider whether a plaintiff has satisfied the requirement when filing suit, but Article III demands that an "actual controversy" persist throughout all stages of litigation. That means that standing "must be met by persons seeking appellate review, just as it must be met by persons appearing in courts of first instance." We therefore must decide whether petitioners had standing to appeal the District Court's order. Respondents initiated this case in the District Court against the California officials responsible for enforcing Proposition 8. The parties do not contest that respondents had Article III standing to do so. Each couple expressed a desire to marry and obtain "official sanction" from the State, which was unavailable to them given the declaration in Proposition 8 that "marriage" in California is solely between a man and a woman. After the District Court declared Proposition 8 unconstitutional and enjoined the state officials named as defendants from enforcing it, however, the inquiry under Article III changed. Respondents no longer had any injury to redress—they had won—and the state officials chose not to appeal.

The only individuals who sought to appeal that order were petitioners, who had intervened in the District Court. But the District Court had not ordered them to do or refrain from doing anything. To have standing, a litigant must seek relief for an injury that affects him in a "personal and individual way." He must possess a "direct stake in the outcome" of the case. Here, however, petitioners had no "direct stake" in the outcome of their appeal. Their only interest in having the District Court order reversed was to vindicate the constitutional validity of a generally applicable California law.

We have repeatedly held that such a "generalized grievance," no matter how sincere, is insufficient to confer standing. A litigant "raising only a generally available grievance about government—claiming only harm to his and every citizen's interest in proper application of the Constitution and laws, and seeking relief that no more directly and tangibly benefits him than it does the public at large—does not state an Article III case or controversy."

Petitioners argue that the California Constitution and its election laws give them a "'unique,' 'special,' and 'distinct' role in the initiative process—"one 'involving both authority and responsibilities that differ from other supporters of the measure.'" True enough—but only when it comes to the process of enacting the law. Upon submitting the proposed initiative to the attorney general, petitioners became the official "proponents" of Proposition 8. As such, they were responsible for collecting the signatures required to qualify the measure for the ballot. After those signatures were collected, the proponents alone had the right to file the measure with election officials to put it on the ballot. Petitioners also possessed control over the arguments in favor of the initiative that would appear in California's ballot pamphlets.

But once Proposition 8 was approved by the voters, the measure became "a duly enacted constitutional amendment or statute." Petitioners have no role—special or otherwise—in the enforcement of Proposition 8. They therefore have no "personal stake" in defending its enforcement that is distinguishable from the general interest of every citizen of California. Article III standing "is not to be placed in the hands of 'concerned bystanders,' who will use it simply as a 'vehicle for the vindication of value interests.'" No matter how deeply committed petitioners may be to upholding Proposition 8 or how "zealous [their] advocacy," that is not a "particularized" interest sufficient to create a case or controversy under Article III. . . .

Without a judicially cognizable interest of their own, petitioners attempt to invoke that of someone else. They assert that even if they have no cognizable interest in appealing the District Court's judgment, the State of California does, and they may assert that interest on the State's behalf. It is, however, a "fundamental restriction on our authority" that "[i]n the ordinary course, a litigant must assert his or her own legal rights and interests, and cannot rest a claim to relief on the legal rights or interests of third parties." There are "certain, limited exceptions" to that rule. But even when we have allowed litigants to assert the interests of others, the litigants themselves still "must have suffered an injury in fact, thus giving [them] a sufficiently concrete interest in the outcome of the issue in dispute." . . .

The dissent eloquently recounts the California Supreme Court's reasons for deciding that state law authorizes petitioners to defend Proposition 8. We do not "disrespect[ ]" or "disparage[ ]" those reasons. Nor do we question California's sovereign right to maintain an initiative process, or the right of initiative proponents to defend their initiatives in California courts, where Article III does not apply. But as the dissent acknowledges, standing in federal court is a question of federal law, not state law. And no matter its reasons, the fact that a State thinks a private party should have standing to seek relief for a generalized grievance cannot override our settled law to the contrary. . . .

We have never before upheld the standing of a private party to defend the constitutionality of a state statute when state officials have chosen not to. We decline to do so for the first time here. here.

Because petitioners have not satisfied their burden to demonstrate standing to appeal the judgment of the District Court, the Ninth Circuit was without jurisdiction to consider the appeal. The judgment of the Ninth Circuit is vacated, and the case is remanded with instructions to dismiss the appeal for lack of jurisdiction.

☐ *Justice KENNEDY, with whom Justice THOMAS, Justice ALITO, and Justice SOTOMAYOR join, dissenting.*

The Court's opinion is correct to state, and the Supreme Court of California was careful to acknowledge, that a proponent's standing to defend an initiative in federal court is a question of federal law. Proper resolution of the justiciability question requires, in this case, a threshold determination of state law. The state-law question is how California defines and elaborates the status and authority of an initiative's proponents who seek to intervene in court to defend the initiative after its adoption by the electorate. Those state-law issues have been addressed in a meticulous and unanimous opinion by the Supreme Court of California.

Under California law, a proponent has the authority to appear in court and assert the State's interest in defending an enacted initiative when the public officials charged with that duty refuse to do so. The State deems such an appearance essential to the integrity of its initiative process. Yet the Court today concludes that this state-defined status and this state-conferred right fall short of meeting federal requirements because the proponents cannot point to a formal delegation of authority that tracks the requirements of the Restatement of Agency. But the State Supreme Court's definition of proponents' powers is binding on this Court. And that definition is fully sufficient to establish the standing and adversity that are requisites for justiciability under Article III of the United States Constitution.

In my view Article III does not require California, when deciding who may appear in court to defend an initiative on its behalf, to comply with the Restatement of Agency or with this Court's view of how a State should make its laws or structure its government. The Court's reasoning does not take into account the fundamental principles or the practical dynamics of the initiative system in California, which uses this mechanism to control and to bypass public officials—the same officials who would not defend the initiative, an injury the Court now leaves unremedied. The Court's decision also has implications for the 26 other States that use an initiative or popular referendum system and which, like California, may choose to have initiative proponents stand in for the State when public officials decline to defend an initiative in litigation. In my submission, the Article III requirement for a justiciable case or controversy does not prevent proponents from having their day in court.

These are the premises for this respectful dissent. . . .

■ THE DEVELOPMENT OF LAW

Class-Action Suits

The Roberts Court has limited the filing of class-action lawsuits in a number of ways (see also The Development of Law box in Vols. 1 and 2, Ch. 1). In *AT&T Mobility v. Concepcion*, 131 S.Ct. 1740 (2011), a bare majority held that a California law was preempted by the Federal Arbitration Act (FAA), which governs arbitration agreements in order to "facilitate streamlined proceedings" in resolving individual disputes. Under California's law class arbitration was permitted, but the majority struck down that law for running afoul of the federal statute. Writing for the majority, Justice Scalia observed that "Requiring the availability of classwide arbitration interferes with fundamental attributes of arbitration and thus creates a scheme inconsistent with the FAA." The Concepcions had signed with AT&T Mobility for a "free" cell phone but were charged $30.22 in fees and sales tax, and in turn sought class-action arbitration of their dispute over the charges. Justices Breyer, Ginsburg, Sotomayor, and Kagan dissented.

A bare majority, however, upheld a class-action suit against California prison officials for violating the Eighth Amendment due to prison overcrowding and the conditions of inmates in *Brown v. Plata*, 131 S.Ct. 1910 (2011) (further discussed below in Vol. 2, Ch. 10).

In a widely watched case involving the largest "class action" suit ever, *Wal-Mart Stores, Inc. v. Dukes*, 131 S.Ct. 2541 (2011), the Court overturned the certification of a nationwide class of some 1.5 million female employees of

Wal-Mart, who claimed that the company systematically discriminated against them in violation of the Civil Rights Act of 1964. Writing for the Court, Justice Scalia held that such a class was too large and inconsistent with the Federal Rule of Civil Procedure 23(a). Wal-Mart has some 3,400 stores across the country—each with its own managers—and therefore was entitled to individual determinations of discrimination and employees' eligibility for back pay. In other words, Rule 23(a) requires showing a commonality shared by each member of the class and a single indivisible remedy that provides the same relief to each class member. The Court did not reach the merits of the employees' claim, and individual women may sue over alleged discrimination, though in many instances that may prove too costly. Justice GINSBURG, joined by Justices BREYER, SOTOMAYOR, and KAGAN, agreed that the section of Rule 23 that permits class-action requests for injunctions or declaratory judgments does not generally allow claims solely for monetary payments, but otherwise dissented. In their view, the women's lawyers had presented enough evidence "that gender bias suffused Wal-Mart's company culture."

A bare majority of the Roberts Court continued its movement toward further limiting taxpayers' standing in *Valley Forge Christian College v. Americans United for Separation of Church and State, Inc.*, 454 U.S. 464 (1982), and *Hein v. Freedom from Religion Foundation, Inc.*, 551 U.S. 587 (2007)—both excerpted in Vols. 1 and 2, Ch. 2), and the watershed ruling in *Flast v. Cohen*, 392 U.S. 83 (1968) (excerpted in Vols. 1 and 2, Ch. 2), which had extended taxpayer standing to challenge legislation appropriating funds for religious schools. Sharply limiting *Flast* in writing for the Court, Justice Kennedy drew a bright line between taxpayer challenges to state appropriations for private religious schools and programs that give taxpayers dollar-for-dollar tax credits on their state taxes for contributions to nonprofit groups that provide scholarships to private schools, including religious schools. In *Arizona Christian School Tuition Organization v. Winn* (2011) (excerpted below), Justice Kennedy held that while taxpayers under *Flast* had standing to challenge appropriations aiding religious schools under the First Amendment (dis)establishment clause, they did not have standing to challenge tax credit programs that permitted contributions to aid religious schools. He did so on the theory that the subsidy for scholarships was not actually from state tax revenues but from donations of taxpayers who then received tax credits. In a concurring opinion, Justice Scalia, joined by Justice Thomas, would have overturned *Flast*. Justice Kagan filed a dissenting opinion, joined by Justices Ginsburg, Breyer, and Sotomayor.

However, the Court unanimously held that individuals have standing, if they meet the requirements of bringing an actual "case or controversy" under Article III, to challenge the constitutionality of federal laws based on a claim that they violate states' sovereignty under the Tenth Amendment, in *Bond v. United States*, 131 S.Ct. 2355 (2011).

In its 2012–2013 term the Court considered whether lawyers, journalists, and international organizations who work with foreign nationals have standing to challenge the constitutionality of 2008 amendments to the Foreign Intelligence Surveillance Act that expanded the federal government's power to intercept emails, telephone conversations, and other global communications, in searching for terrorist threats. Although the act authorizes targeting only foreign nationals, communications involving Americans may be monitored. A panel of the U.S. Court of Appeals for the Second Circuit held that the law could be challenged on its face and an evenly split *en banc* Second Circuit refused to reconsider that decision. In its appeal in *Clapper v. Amnesty International*, 133 S.Ct. 1138 (2013), the Obama administration contends that the suit is too abstract, and that none of the parties challenging the amendments have shown that their communications were actually overheard by electronic wiretaps. The Court agreed and dismissed the suit as too speculative to establish standing to sue.

Arizona Christian School Tuition Organization v. Winn
131 S.Ct. 1436 (2011)

Since 1999 Arizona has provided tax credits for contributions to school tuition organizations (or STOs). Under the program, taxpayers have the choice of making contributions to secular or religious STOs and receiving tax credits. STOs provide scholarships to students attending private schools, primarily Catholic schools. A group of Arizona taxpayers challenged the STO tax credit as violation of the First Amendment's (dis)establishment clause. After the state supreme court rejected a similar suit, the taxpayers filed suit in federal court. In order to do so they had to demonstrate their standing to sue based on a direct harm of a violation of the (dis)establishment clause, such as a mandatory prayer in public school classes. On remand, the Arizona Christian School Tuition Organization intervened and the district court once again dismissed the suit, but the Court of Appeals for the Ninth Circuit reversed and held that the taxpayers had standing to bring the suit under *Flast v. Cohen* (1968). That decision was appealed and the Supreme Court granted review.

The appellate court's decision was reversed by a bare majority. Justice Kennedy delivered the opinion for the Court and Justice Scalia filed a concurring opinion, joined by Justice Thomas, contending that *Flast* should be overturned. Justice Kagen filed a dissenting opinion, which Justices Ginsburg, Breyer, and Sotomayor joined.

☐ *Justice KENNEDY delivered the opinion of the Court.*

To state a case or controversy under Article III, a plaintiff must establish standing. The minimum constitutional requirements for standing were explained in *Lujan v. Defenders of Wildlife*, 504 U.S. 555 (1992). "First, the plaintiff must have suffered an 'injury in fact'—an invasion of a legally protected interest which is (a) concrete and particularized, and (b) 'actual or imminent, not "conjectural" or "hypothetical."' Second, there must be a causal connection between the injury and the conduct complained of—the injury has to be 'fairly . . . trace[able] to the challenged action of the defendant, and not . . . th[e] result [of] the independent action of some third party not before the court.' Third, it must be 'likely,' as opposed to merely 'speculative,' that the injury will be 'redressed by a favorable decision.'" In requiring a particular injury, the Court meant "that the injury must affect the plaintiff in a personal and individual way." The question now before the Court is whether respondents, the plaintiffs in the trial court, satisfy the requisite elements of standing.

Respondents suggest that their status as Arizona taxpayers provides them with standing to challenge the STO tax credit. Absent special circumstances, however, standing cannot be based on a plaintiff's mere status as a taxpayer. This Court has rejected the general proposition that an individual who has paid taxes has a "continuing, legally cognizable interest in ensuring that those funds are not used by the Government in a way that violates the Constitution." *Hein v. Freedom From Religion Foundation, Inc.*, 551 U.S. 587 (2007). This precept has been referred to as the rule against taxpayer standing.

The doctrinal basis for the rule was discussed in *Frothingham v. Mellon*, 262 U.S. 447 (1923). There, a taxpayer-plaintiff had alleged that certain federal expenditures were in excess of congressional authority under the Constitution. The plaintiff argued that she had standing to raise her claim because she had an interest in the Government Treasury and because the allegedly unconstitutional expenditure of Government funds would affect her personal tax liability. The Court rejected those arguments. The "effect upon future taxation, of any payment out of funds," was too "remote, fluctuating and uncertain" to give rise to a case or controversy. And the taxpayer-plaintiff's "interest in the moneys of the Treasury," the Court recognized, was necessarily "shared with millions of others." As a consequence, *Frothingham* held that the taxpayer-plaintiff had not presented a "judicial controversy" appropriate for resolution in federal court but rather a "matter of public . . . concern" that could be pursued only through the political process.

In holdings consistent with *Frothingham* and *Doremus* [*v. Board of Education of Hawthorne*, 342 U.S. 429 (1959)], more recent decisions have explained that claims of taxpayer standing rest on unjustifiable economic and political speculation. When a government expends resources or declines to impose a tax, its budget does not necessarily suffer. On the contrary, the purpose of many governmental expenditures and tax benefits is "to spur economic activity, which in turn increases government revenues." . . .

These well-established principles apply to the present cases. Respondents may be right that Arizona's STO tax credits have an estimated annual value of over $50 million. The education of its young people is, of course, one of the State's principal missions and responsibilities; and the consequent costs will make up a significant portion of the state budget. That, however, is just the beginning of the analysis.

By helping students obtain scholarships to private schools, both religious and secular, the STO program might relieve the burden placed on Arizona's public schools. The result could be an immediate and permanent cost savings for the State. . . .

The primary contention of respondents, of course, is that, despite the general rule that taxpayers lack standing to object to expenditures alleged to be unconstitutional, their suit falls within the exception established by *Flast v. Cohen*. It must be noted at the outset that, as this Court has explained, *Flast*'s holding provides a "narrow exception" to "the general rule against taxpayer standing." *Bowen v. Kendrick*, 487 U.S. 589 (1988). . . .

Respondents contend that . . . the tax credit is, for *Flast* purposes, best understood as a government expenditure. That is incorrect.

It is easy to see that tax credits and governmental expenditures can have similar economic consequences, at least for beneficiaries whose tax liability is sufficiently large to take full advantage of the credit. Yet tax credits and governmental expenditures do not both implicate individual taxpayers in sectarian activities. A dissenter whose tax dollars are "extracted and spent" knows that he has in some small measure been made to contribute to an establishment in violation of conscience. In that instance the taxpayer's direct and particular connection with the establishment does not depend on economic speculation or political conjecture. The connection would exist even if the conscientious dissenter's tax liability were unaffected or reduced. When the government declines to impose a tax, by contrast, there is no such connection between dissenting taxpayer and alleged establishment. Any financial injury remains speculative. And awarding some citizens a tax credit allows other citizens to retain control over their own funds in accordance with their own consciences.

The distinction between governmental expenditures and tax credits refutes respondents' assertion of standing. When Arizona taxpayers choose to contribute to STOs, they spend their own money, not money the State has collected from respondents or from other taxpayers. . . . Furthermore, respondents cannot satisfy the requirements of causation and redressability. When the government collects and spends taxpayer money, governmental choices are responsible for the transfer of wealth. In that case a resulting subsidy of religious activity is, for purposes of *Flast*, traceable to the government's expenditures. . . . Here, by contrast, contributions result from the decisions of private taxpayers regarding their own funds. Private citizens create private STOs; STOs choose beneficiary schools; and taxpayers then contribute to STOs. . . .

Few exercises of the judicial power are more likely to undermine public confidence in the neutrality and integrity of the Judiciary than one which casts the Court in the role of a Council of Revision, conferring on itself the power to invalidate laws at the behest of anyone who disagrees with them. In an era of frequent litigation, class actions, sweeping injunctions with prospective effect, and continuing jurisdiction to enforce judicial remedies, courts must be more careful to insist on the formal rules of standing, not less so. Making the Article III standing inquiry all the more necessary are the significant implications of constitutional litigation, which can result in rules of wide applicability that are beyond Congress' power to change. . . .

◻ *Justice KAGAN, with whom Justice GINSBURG, Justice BREYER, and Justice SOTOMAYOR join, dissenting.*

Beginning in *Flast v. Cohen* and continuing in case after case for over four decades, this Court and others have exercised jurisdiction to decide taxpayer-initiated challenges not materially different from this one. Not every suit has succeeded on the merits, or should have. But every taxpayer-plaintiff has had her day in court to contest the government's financing of religious activity.

Today, the Court breaks from this precedent by refusing to hear taxpayers' claims that the government has unconstitutionally subsidized religion through its tax system. These litigants lack standing, the majority holds, because the funding of religion they challenge comes from a tax credit, rather than an appropriation. A tax credit, the Court asserts, does not injure objecting taxpayers, because it "does not extract and spend [their] funds in service of an establishment."

This novel distinction in standing law between appropriations and tax expenditures has as little basis in principle as it has in our precedent. Cash grants and targeted tax breaks are means of accomplishing the same government objective—to provide financial support to select individuals or organizations. Taxpayers who oppose state aid of religion have equal reason to protest whether that aid flows from the one form of subsidy or the other. Either way, the government has financed the religious activity. And so either way, taxpayers should be able to challenge the subsidy.

Still worse, the Court's arbitrary distinction threatens to eliminate all occasions for a taxpayer to contest the government's monetary support of religion. Precisely because appropriations and tax breaks can achieve identical objectives, the government can easily substitute one for the other. Today's opinion thus enables the government to end-run *Flast*'s guarantee of access to the Judiciary. From now on, the government need follow just one simple rule—subsidize through the tax system—to preclude taxpayer challenges to state funding of religion. . . . Because I believe these challenges warrant consideration on the merits, I respectfully dissent from the Court's decision. . . .

B | *The Court's Docket and Screening Cases*

■ INSIDE THE COURT

The Business of the Supreme Court in the 2012–2013 Term★

SUBJECT OF COURT OPINIONS	SUMMARY	PLENARY
Admiralty		1
Antitrust		1
Bankruptcy		1
Bill of Rights (other than rights of accused) and Equal Protection	1	11
Commerce Clause		
1. Constitutionality and construction of federal regulation		4
2. Constitutionality of state regulation		2
Common Law		
Miscellaneous Statutory Construction	2	20
Due process		
1. Economic interests		
2. Procedure and rights of accused	1	3
3. Substantive due process (noneconomic)		
Impairment of Contract and Just Compensation		
International Law, War, and Peace		
Jurisdiction, Procedure, and Practice	2	22
Land Legislation		
Native Americans		1
Patents, Copyright, and Trademarks		3
Other Suits against the Government		4
Suits by States		
Taxation (federal and state)		1
Totals	6	74

★Note: The classification of cases is that of the author and necessarily invites differences of opinion as to the dominant issue in some cases. The table includes opinions in cases whether decided summarily or given plenary consideration but not cases summarily disposed of by simple orders, opinions dissenting from the denial of review, and those dismissing cases as improvidently granted.

H | *Opinion Days and Communicating Decisions*

■ Inside the Court

*Opinion Writing during the 2012–2013 Term**

OPINIONS	MAJORITY	CONCURRING	DISSENTING	SEPARATE	TOTALS
Per Curiam	7				7
Roberts	8	2	6	1	17
Scalia	8	5	10	1	24
Kennedy	8	4	1		13
Thomas	8	10	6		24
Ginsburg	9	1	7		17
Breyer	8	5	4		17
Alito	8	6	7		21
Sotomayor	8	3	4		15
Kagan	8	2	3		13
Totals	80	38	48	2	168

*Note that court opinions disposing of two or more companion cases are counted only once here. In addition, this table includes opinions in cases disposed of either summarily or upon plenary consideration, but does not include cases summarily disposed of by simple orders, dismissed as improvidently granted, and concurring or dissenting opinions from the denial of *certiorari*. In *Comcast v. Behrend* (2013), Justices Ginsburg and Breyer issued an unusual joint dissenting opinion, joined by Justices Sotomayor and Kagan, and is counted twice.

4

The President as Chief Executive in Domestic Affairs

By a six to three vote the Roberts Court reaffirmed and extended the so-called *Chevron* doctrine, *Chevron v. Natural Resources Defense Council*, 467 U.S. 837 (1984) (discussed in Vol. 1, Ch. 4), of judicial deference to federal agencies' interpretation of their statutory authority to include interpretation of their jurisdiction in *City of Arlington v. FCC*, 133 S.Ct. 1863 (2013). Writing for the majority, Justice Scalia held that jurisdictional and nonjurisdictional matters were "a mirage." By contrast, dissenting Chief Justice Roberts, joined by Justices Kennedy and Alito, warned of "the danger posed by the growing power of the administrative state" that permits "hundreds of federal agencies poking into every nook and cranny of daily life."

B | *Appointment and Removal Powers*

In its 2013–2014 term the Court will consider the scope of the President's power to make recess appointments in *National Labor Relations Board v. Canning* (No. 12-1281). More specifically, (1) whether the President's recess-appointment power may be exercised during a recess that occurs within a session of the Senate, or instead is limited to recesses occurring between enumerated sessions of the Senate, and (2) whether the President's recess-appointment power may be used to fill vacancies that exist during a recess, or is limited to vacancies that first arose during a recess. In addition, the Court has asked counsel to address the question (3) of whether the President may exercise his power when the Senate is in recess but convenes for three-day *pro forma* sessions?

6

CONGRESS: LEGISLATIVE, TAXING, AND SPENDING POWERS

C | *From the New Deal Crisis to the Administrative State*

By a four-one-four vote the Roberts Court upheld the major controversial provision of the Patient Protection and Affordable Care Act of 2010 in *National Federation of Independent Business v. Sebelius* (excerpted below in Section D). Chief Justice Roberts delivered the opinion of the Court, holding that Congress exceeded its power under the Commerce Clause but upholding the "individual mandate" under Congress's power to tax and spend for the general welfare. Chief Justice Roberts also struck down the extension of Medicaid and other provisions. In a separate opinion, Justice Ginsburg, joined by Justices Breyer, Sotomayor, and Kagan, would have upheld all of the law's provisions and held that the "individual mandate" was within Congress's power to regulate interstate commerce. In an unsigned dissenting opinion, Justices Scalia, Kennedy, Thomas, and Alito would have struck down the law in its entirety. Justice Thomas also filed a separate dissenting opinion.

D | *Taxing and Spending Powers*

National Federation of Independent Business v. Sebelius
131 S.Ct. 2566 (2012)

In 2010 Congress enacted the Patient Protection and Affordable Care Act, aimed at increasing the number of Americans covered by health insurance and decreasing the cost of health care. The act's ten titles include 900 pages and contain hundreds of provisions. Two principle provisions, commonly referred to as the "individual mandate" and an extension of Medicaid, were immediately challenged by 26 states and numerous business organizations. The "individual mandate" requires most Americans to maintain "minimum essential" health insurance coverage. If individuals do not receive health insurance through their employer, they must purchase insurance from a private company. Beginning in 2014, those who do not comply must make a "[s]hared responsibility payment," or penalty or tax, to the federal government. In 2016 that penalty or tax will be 2.5 percent of an individual's household income, but no less than $695 and no more than the average yearly premium for insurance that covers 60 percent of the cost of ten specified services, such as prescription drugs and hospitalization. A federal district court struck the law down in its entirety. On appeal the Court of Appeals for the Eleventh Circuit affirmed in part and reversed in part, holding that the "individual mandate" exceeded Congress's power under the Commerce Clause and that it did not impose a tax, and thus could not be upheld under Congress's power to tax and spend. Other courts of appeals also heard constitutional challenges to the law and on appeal the Supreme Court consolidated the cases and heard an extraordinary six hours of oral arguments over the law.

The appellate court's decision was reversed and affirmed in part. Chief Justice Roberts delivered the opinion of the Court, holding that Congress exceeded its power under the Commerce Clause but upholding the "individual mandate" under Congress's power to tax and spend for the general welfare. Chief Justice Roberts also struck down the extension of Medicaid and other provisions. In a separate opinion, Justice Ginsburg, joined by Justices Breyer, Sotomayor, and Kagan, would have upheld all of the law's provisions and held that the "individual mandate" was within Congress's power to regulate interstate commerce. In an unsigned dissenting opinion, Justices Scalia, Kennedy, Thomas, and Alito would have struck down the law in its entirety. Justice Thomas also filed a separate dissenting opinion.

☐ *CHIEF JUSTICE ROBERTS announced the judgment of the Court and delivered the opinion of the Court with respect to Parts I, II, and III–C, an opinion with respect to Part IV, in which Justice BREYER and Justice KAGAN join, and an opinion with respect to Parts III–A, III–B, and III–D.*

Today we resolve constitutional challenges to two provisions of the Patient Protection and Affordable Care Act of 2010: the individual mandate, which requires individuals to purchase a health insurance policy providing a minimum level of coverage; and the Medicaid expansion, which gives funds to the States on the condition that they provide specified health care to all citizens whose income falls below a certain threshold. We do not consider whether the Act embodies sound policies. That judgment is entrusted to the Nation's elected leaders. We ask only whether Congress has the power under the Constitution to enact the challenged provisions. . . .

This case concerns two powers that the Constitution does grant the Federal Government, but which must be read carefully to avoid creating a general federal authority akin to the police power. The Constitution authorizes Congress to "regulate Commerce with foreign Nations, and among the several States, and with the Indian Tribes." Art. I, Sec. 8, cl. 3. Our precedents read that to mean that Congress may regulate "the channels of interstate commerce," "persons or things in interstate commerce," and "those activities that substantially affect interstate commerce." [*United States v.*] *Morrison*, 529 U.S. 598 (2000). The power over activities that substantially affect interstate commerce can be expansive. That power has been held to authorize federal regulation of such seemingly local matters as a farmer's decision to grow wheat for himself and his livestock, and a loan shark's extortionate collections from a neighborhood butcher shop. See *Wickard v. Filburn*, 317 U.S. 111 (1942); *Perez v. United States*, 402 U.S. 146 (1971).

Congress may also "lay and collect Taxes, Duties, Imposts and Excises, to pay the Debts and provide for the common Defence and general Welfare of the United States." U. S. Const., Art. I, Sec. 8, cl. 1. Put simply, Congress may tax and spend. This grant gives the Federal Government considerable influence even in areas where it cannot directly regulate. The Federal Government may enact a tax on an activity that it cannot authorize, forbid, or otherwise control. See, e.g., *License Tax Cases*, 5 Wall. 462 (1867). And in exercising its spending power, Congress may offer funds to the States, and may condition those offers on compliance with specified conditions. These offers may well induce the States to adopt policies that the Federal Government itself could not impose. See, e.g., *South Dakota v. Dole*, 483 U S. 203 (1987) (conditioning federal highway funds on States raising their drinking age to 21). . . .

Our permissive reading of these powers is explained in part by a general reticence to invalidate the acts of the Nation's elected leaders. Members of this Court are vested with the authority to interpret the law; we possess neither the expertise nor the prerogative to make policy judgments. . . .

Our deference in matters of policy cannot, however, become abdication in matters of law. Our respect for Congress's policy judgments thus can never extend so far as to disavow restraints on federal power that the Constitution carefully constructed. And there can be no question that it is the responsibility of this Court to enforce the limits on federal power by striking down acts of Congress that transgress those limits. *Marbury v. Madison*, 1 Cranch 137 (1803). . . .

■ III

The Government advances two theories for the proposition that Congress had constitutional authority to enact the individual mandate. First, the Government argues that Congress had the power to enact the mandate under the Commerce Clause. Under that theory, Congress may order individuals to buy health insurance because the failure to do so affects interstate commerce, and could undercut the Affordable Care Act's other reforms. Second, the Government argues that if the commerce power does not support the mandate, we should nonetheless uphold it as an exercise of Congress's power to tax. According to the Government, even if Congress lacks the power to direct individuals to buy insurance, the only effect of the individual mandate is to raise taxes on those who do not do so, and thus the law may be upheld as a tax.

The Government contends that the individual mandate is within Congress's power because the failure to purchase insurance "has a substantial and deleterious effect on interstate commerce" by creating the cost-shifting problem. Congress has broad authority under the Clause. . . .

Given its expansive scope, it is no surprise that Congress has employed the commerce power in a wide variety of ways to address the pressing needs of the time. But Congress has never attempted to rely on that power to compel individuals not engaged in commerce to purchase an unwanted product. . . . The power to regulate commerce presupposes the existence of commercial activity to be regulated. If the power to "regulate" something included the power to create it, many of the provisions in the Constitution would be superfluous. . . .

The individual mandate, however, does not regulate existing commercial activity. It instead compels individuals to become active in commerce by purchasing a product, on the ground that their failure to do so affects interstate commerce. Construing the Commerce Clause to permit Congress to regulate individuals precisely because they are doing nothing would open a new and potentially vast domain to congressional authority. Every day individuals do not do an infinite number of things. In some cases they decide not to do something; in others they simply fail to do it. Allowing Congress to justify federal regulation by pointing to the effect of inaction on commerce would bring countless decisions an individual could potentially make within the scope of federal regulation, and—under the Government's theory—empower Congress to make those decisions for him.

Applying the Government's logic to the familiar case of *Wickard v. Filburn* shows how far that logic would carry us from the notion of a government of limited powers. In *Wickard*, the Court famously upheld a federal penalty imposed on a farmer for growing wheat for consumption on his own farm. That amount of wheat caused the farmer to exceed his quota under a program designed to support the price of wheat by limiting supply. The Court rejected the farmer's argument that growing wheat for home consumption was beyond the reach of the commerce power. It did so on the ground that the farmer's decision to grow wheat for his own use allowed him to avoid purchasing wheat in the market. That decision, when considered in the aggregate along with similar decisions of others, would have had a substantial effect on the interstate market for wheat.

Wickard has long been regarded as "perhaps the most far reaching example of Commerce Clause authority over intrastate activity," but the Government's theory in this case would go much further. Under *Wickard* it is within Congress's power to regulate the market for wheat by supporting its price.

But price can be supported by increasing demand as well as by decreasing supply. The aggregated decisions of some consumers not to purchase wheat have a substantial effect on the price of wheat, just as decisions not to purchase health insurance have on the price of insurance. Congress can therefore command that those not buying wheat do so, just as it argues here that it may command that those not buying health insurance do so. The farmer in *Wickard* was at least actively engaged in the production of wheat, and the Government could regulate that activity because of its effect on commerce. The Government's theory here would effectively override that limitation, by establishing that individuals may be regulated under the Commerce Clause whenever enough of them are not doing something the Government would have them do.

Indeed, the Government's logic would justify a mandatory purchase to solve almost any problem. To consider a different example in the health care market, many Americans do not eat a balanced diet. That group makes up a larger percentage of the total population than those without health insurance. The failure of that group to have a healthy diet increases health care costs, to a greater extent than the failure of the uninsured to purchase insurance. Those increased costs are borne in part by other Americans who must pay more, just as the uninsured shift costs to the insured. Congress addressed the insurance problem by ordering everyone to buy insurance. Under the Government's theory, Congress could address the diet problem by ordering everyone to buy vegetables.

People, for reasons of their own, often fail to do things that would be good for them or good for society. Those failures—joined with the similar failures of others—can readily have a substantial effect on interstate commerce. Under the Government's logic, that authorizes Congress to use its commerce power to compel citizens to act as the Government would have them act.

That is not the country the Framers of our Constitution envisioned. James Madison explained that the Commerce Clause was "an addition which few oppose and from which no apprehensions are entertained." *The Federalist* No. 45. While Congress's authority under the Commerce Clause has of course expanded with the growth of the national economy, our cases have "always recognized that the power to regulate commerce, though broad indeed, has limits." *Maryland v. Wirtz*, 392 U S. 183 (1968). The Government's theory would erode those limits, permitting Congress to reach beyond the natural extent of its authority, "everywhere extending the sphere of its activity and drawing all power into its impetuous vortex." *The Federalist* No. 48 (J. Madison). Congress already enjoys vast power to regulate much of what we do. Accepting the Government's theory would give Congress the same license to regulate what we do not do, fundamentally changing the relation between the citizen and the Federal Government. . . .

The proposition that Congress may dictate the conduct of an individual today because of prophesied future activity finds no support in our precedent. We have said that Congress can anticipate the effects on commerce of an economic activity. See, e.g., *Heart of Atlanta Motel, Inc. v. United States*, 379 U.S. 241 (1964) (prohibiting discrimination by hotel operators); *Katzenbach v. McClung*, 379 U.S. 294 (1964) (prohibiting discrimination by restaurant owners). But we have never permitted Congress to anticipate that activity itself in order to regulate individuals not currently engaged in commerce. . . .

The Government next contends that Congress has the power under the Necessary and Proper Clause to enact the individual mandate because the mandate is an "integral part of a comprehensive scheme of economic regulation"—the guaranteed-issue and community-rating insurance reforms. . . .

As our jurisprudence under the Necessary and Proper Clause has developed, we have been very deferential to Congress's determination that a regulation is "necessary." We have thus upheld laws that are "'convenient, or useful' or 'conducive' to the authority's 'beneficial exercise.'" But we have also carried out our responsibility to declare unconstitutional those laws that undermine the structure of government established by the Constitution. Rather, they are, "in the words of *The Federalist*, 'merely acts of usurpation' which 'deserve to be treated as such.'"

Applying these principles, the individual mandate cannot be sustained under the Necessary and Proper Clause as an essential component of the insurance reforms. . . .

The Government relies primarily on our decision in *Gonzales v. Raich*, 545 U.S. 1 (2005). In *Raich*, we considered "comprehensive legislation to regulate the interstate market" in marijuana. Certain individuals sought an exemption from that regulation on the ground that they engaged in only intrastate possession and consumption. We denied any exemption, on the ground that marijuana is a fungible commodity, so that any marijuana could be readily diverted into the interstate market. Congress's attempt to regulate the interstate market for marijuana would therefore have been substantially undercut if it could not also regulate intrastate possession and consumption. Accordingly, we recognized that "Congress was acting well within its authority" under the Necessary and Proper Clause even though its "regulation ensnare[d] some purely intrastate activity."

Just as the individual mandate cannot be sustained as a law regulating the substantial effects of the failure to purchase health insurance, neither can it be upheld as a "necessary and proper" component of the insurance reforms. The commerce power thus does not authorize the mandate.

That is not the end of the matter. Because the Commerce Clause does not support the individual mandate, it is necessary to turn to the Government's second argument: that the mandate may be upheld as within Congress's enumerated power to "lay and collect Taxes." . . .

Under the mandate, if an individual does not maintain health insurance, the only consequence is that he must make an additional payment to the IRS when he pays his taxes. . . .

It is of course true that the Act describes the payment as a "penalty," not a "tax." But while that label is fatal to the application of the Anti-Injunction Act, it does not determine whether the payment may be viewed as an exercise of Congress's taxing power. It is up to Congress whether to apply the Anti-Injunction Act to any particular statute, so it makes sense to be guided by Congress's choice of label on that question. That choice does not, however, control whether an exaction is within Congress's constitutional power to tax.

Our precedent reflects this. . . . We have similarly held that exactions not labeled taxes nonetheless were authorized by Congress's power to tax. In the *License Tax Cases*, for example, we held that federal licenses to sell liquor and lottery tickets—for which the licensee had to pay a fee—could be sustained as exercises of the taxing power. And in *New York v. United States*, [505 U.S. 144 (1992)] we upheld as a tax a "surcharge" on out-of-state nuclear waste shipments, a portion of which was paid to the Federal Treasury. . . .

The same analysis here suggests that the shared responsibility payment may for constitutional purposes be considered a tax, not a penalty: First, for most Americans the amount due will be far less than the price of insurance, and, by statute, it can never be more. It may often be a reasonable financial decision to make the payment rather than purchase insurance. [Moreover] the payment is collected solely by the IRS through the normal means of taxation—except that the Service is not allowed to use those means most suggestive of a punitive sanction, such as criminal prosecution. . . .

In distinguishing penalties from taxes, this Court has explained that "if the concept of penalty means anything, it means punishment for an unlawful act or omission." *United States v. Reorganized CF&I Fabricators of Utah, Inc.*, 518 U.S. 213 (1996). While the individual mandate clearly aims to induce the purchase of health insurance, it need not be read to declare that failing to do so is unlawful. Neither the Act nor any other law attaches negative legal consequences to not buying health insurance, beyond requiring a payment to the IRS. The Government agrees with that reading, confirming that if someone chooses to pay rather than obtain health insurance, they have fully complied with the law. . . .

Our precedent demonstrates that Congress had the power to impose the exaction in Sec. 5000A under the taxing power, and that Sec. 5000A need not be read to do more than impose a tax. That is sufficient to sustain it. . . .

The Affordable Care Act's requirement that certain individuals pay a financial penalty for not obtaining health insurance may reasonably be characterized as a tax. Because the Constitution permits such a tax, it is not our role to forbid it, or to pass upon its wisdom or fairness. . . .

■ IV

The States also contend that the Medicaid expansion exceeds Congress's authority under the Spending Clause. They claim that Congress is coercing the States to adopt the changes it wants by threatening to withhold all of a State's Medicaid grants, unless the State accepts the new expanded funding and complies with the conditions that come with it. This, they argue, violates the basic principle that the "Federal Government may not compel the States to enact or administer a federal regulatory program." *New York* [*v. United States*].

There is no doubt that the Act dramatically increases state obligations under Medicaid. The current Medicaid program requires States to cover only certain discrete categories of needy individuals—pregnant women, children, needy families, the blind, the elderly, and the disabled. There is no mandatory coverage for most childless adults, and the States typically do not offer any such coverage. The States also enjoy considerable flexibility with respect to the coverage levels for parents of needy families.

The Medicaid provisions of the Affordable Care Act, in contrast, require States to expand their Medicaid programs by 2014 to cover all individuals under the age of 65 with incomes below 133 percent of the federal poverty line. The Act also establishes a new "[e]ssential health benefits" package, which States must provide to all new Medicaid recipients—a level sufficient to satisfy a recipient's obligations under the individual mandate. The Affordable Care Act provides that the Federal Government will pay 100 percent of the costs of covering these newly eligible individuals through 2016. In the following years, the federal payment level gradually decreases, to a minimum of 90 percent. . . .

The Spending Clause grants Congress the power "to pay the Debts and provide for the . . . general Welfare of the United States." We have long recognized that Congress may use this power to grant federal funds to the States, and may condition such a grant upon the States' "taking certain actions that Congress could not require them to take." . . .

At the same time, our cases have recognized limits on Congress's power under the Spending Clause to secure state compliance with federal objectives... For this reason, "the Constitution has never been understood to confer upon Congress the ability to require the States to govern according to Congress' instructions." *New York*. Otherwise the two-government system established by the Framers would give way to a system that vests power in one central government, and individual liberty would suffer.

That insight has led this Court to strike down federal legislation that commandeers a State's legislative or administrative apparatus for federal purposes. See, e.g., *Printz* [*v. United States*], 521 U.S. 898 (1997) (striking down federal legislation compelling state law enforcement officers to perform federally mandated background checks on handgun purchasers); *New York* (invalidating provisions of an Act that would compel a State to either take title to nuclear waste or enact particular state waste regulations). It has also led us to scrutinize Spending Clause legislation to ensure that Congress is not using financial inducements to exert a "power akin to undue influence." *Steward Machine Co. v. Davis*, 301 U.S. 548 (1937). Congress may use its spending power to create incentives for States to act in accordance with federal policies. But when "pressure turns into compulsion," the legislation runs contrary to our system of federalism. That is true whether Congress directly commands a State to regulate or indirectly coerces a State to adopt a federal regulatory system as its own.

Permitting the Federal Government to force the States to implement a federal program would threaten the political accountability key to our federal system. Spending Clause programs do not pose this danger when a State has a legitimate choice whether to accept the federal conditions in exchange for federal funds. In such a situation, state officials can fairly be held politically accountable for choosing to accept or refuse the federal offer. But when the State has no choice, the Federal Government can achieve its objectives without accountability, just as in *New York* and *Printz*. Indeed, this danger is heightened when Congress acts under the Spending Clause, because Congress can use that power to implement federal policy it could not impose directly under its enumerated powers. . . .

As our decision in *Steward Machine* confirms, Congress may attach appropriate conditions to federal taxing and spending programs to preserve its control over the use of federal funds. In the typical case we look to the States to defend their prerogatives by adopting "the simple expedient of not yielding" to federal blandishments when they do not want to embrace the federal policies as their own. The States are separate and independent sovereigns. Sometimes they have to act like it.

The States, however, argue that the Medicaid expansion is far from the typical case. They object that Congress has "crossed the line distinguishing encouragement from coercion," *New York*, in the way it has structured the funding: Instead of simply refusing to grant the new funds to States that will not accept the new conditions, Congress has also threatened to withhold those States' existing Medicaid funds. The States claim that this threat serves no purpose other than to force unwilling States to sign up for the dramatic expansion in health care coverage effected by the Act.

Given the nature of the threat and the programs at issue here, we must agree. . . .

In *South Dakota v. Dole*, [483 U.S. 203 (1987)], we considered a challenge to a federal law that threatened to withhold five percent of a State's federal highway funds if the State did not raise its drinking age to 21. The Court found that the condition was "directly related to one of the main purposes for which highway funds are expended—safe interstate travel." At the same time, the condition was not a restriction on how the highway funds—set aside for specific highway improvement and maintenance efforts—were to be used. . . .

In this case, the financial "inducement" Congress has chosen is much more than "relatively mild encouragement"—it is a gun to the head. Section 1396c of the Medicaid Act provides that if a State's Medicaid plan does not comply with the Act's requirements, the Secretary of Health and Human Services may declare that "further payments will not be made to the State." A State that opts out of the Affordable Care Act's expansion in health care coverage thus stands to lose not merely "a relatively small percentage" of its existing Medicaid funding, but all of it. . . .

The Medicaid expansion, however, accomplishes a shift in kind, not merely degree. The original program was designed to cover medical services for four particular categories of the needy: the disabled, the blind, the elderly, and needy families with dependent children. Previous amendments to Medicaid eligibility merely altered and expanded the boundaries of these categories. Under the Affordable Care Act, Medicaid is transformed into a program to meet the health care needs of the entire nonelderly population with income below 133 percent of the poverty level. It is no longer a program to care for the neediest among us, but rather an element of a comprehensive national plan to provide universal health insurance coverage. . . .

The Affordable Care Act is constitutional in part and unconstitutional in part. The individual mandate cannot be upheld as an exercise of Congress's power under the Commerce Clause. That Clause authorizes Congress to regulate interstate commerce, not to order individuals to engage in it. In this case, however, it is reasonable to construe what Congress has done as increasing taxes on those who have a certain amount of income, but choose to go without health insurance. Such legislation is within Congress's power to tax. As for the Medicaid expansion, that portion of the Affordable Care Act violates the Constitution by threatening existing Medicaid funding. Congress has no authority to order the States to regulate according to its instructions. Congress may offer the States grants and require the States to comply with accompanying conditions, but the States must have a genuine choice whether to accept the offer. The States are given no such choice in this case: They must either accept a basic change in the nature of Medicaid, or risk losing all Medicaid funding. The remedy for that constitutional violation is to preclude the Federal Government from imposing such a sanction. That remedy does not require striking down other portions of the Affordable Care Act. . . .

The judgment of the Court of Appeals for the Eleventh Circuit is affirmed in part and reversed in part.

☐ *Justice GINSBURG, with whom Justice SOTOMAYOR joins, and with whom Justice BREYER and Justice KAGAN join as to Parts I, II, III, and IV, concurring in part, concurring in the judgment in part, and dissenting in part.*

I agree with The Chief Justice that the Anti-Injunction Act does not bar the Court's consideration of this case, and that the minimum coverage provision is a proper exercise of Congress' taxing power. I therefore join Parts I, II, and III–C of The Chief Justice's opinion. Unlike The Chief Justice, however, I would hold, alternatively, that the Commerce Clause authorizes Congress to enact the minimum coverage provision. I would also hold that the Spending Clause permits the Medicaid expansion exactly as Congress enacted it.

■ I

Since 1937, our precedent has recognized Congress's large authority to set the Nation's course in the economic and social welfare realm. See *United States v. Darby*, 312 U.S. 100 (1941) (overruling *Hammer v. Dagenhart*, 247 U.S. 251 (1918), and recognizing that "regulations of commerce which do not infringe some constitutional prohibition are within the plenary power conferred on Congress by the Commerce Clause"); *NLRB v. Jones & Laughlin Steel Corp.*, 301 U.S. 1 (1937) ("[The commerce] power is plenary and may be exerted to protect interstate commerce no matter what the source of the dangers which threaten it." The Chief Justice's crabbed reading of the Commerce Clause harks back to the era in which the Court routinely thwarted Congress' efforts to regulate the national economy in the interest of those who labor to sustain it.

In enacting the Patient Protection and Affordable Care Act (ACA), Congress comprehensively reformed the national market for health-care products and services. By any measure, that market is immense. Collectively, Americans spent $2.5 trillion on health care in 2009, accounting for 17.6% of our Nation's economy. Within the next decade, it is anticipated, spending on health care will nearly double.

The health-care market's size is not its only distinctive feature. Unlike the market for almost any other product or service, the market for medical care is one in which all individuals inevitably participate. Virtually every person residing in the United States, sooner or later, will visit a doctor or other health-care professional. . . .

To manage the risks associated with medical care—its high cost, its unpredictability, and its inevitability—most people in the United States obtain health insurance. Many (approximately 170 million in 2009) are insured by private insurance companies. Others, including those over 65 and certain poor and disabled persons, rely on government-funded insurance programs, notably Medicare and Medicaid. Combined, private health insurers and State and Federal Governments finance almost 85% of the medical care administered to U.S. residents. . . .

The large number of individuals without health insurance, Congress found, heavily burdens the national health-care market. . . . As a consequence, medical-care providers deliver significant amounts of care to the uninsured for which the providers receive no payment. . . .

States cannot resolve the problem of the uninsured on their own. Like Social Security benefits, a universal health-care system, if adopted by an individual State, would be "bait to the needy and dependent elsewhere, encouraging them to migrate and seek a haven of repose." . . .

Aware that a national solution was required, Congress could have taken over the health-insurance market by establishing a tax-and-spend federal program like Social Security. Such a program, commonly referred to as a single-payer system (where the sole payer is the Federal Government), would have left little, if any, room for private enterprise or the States. Instead of going this route, Congress enacted the ACA, a solution that retains a robust role for private insurers and state governments. To make its chosen approach work, however, Congress had to use some new tools, including a requirement that most individuals obtain private health insurance coverage. . . .

In sum, Congress passed the minimum coverage provision as a key component of the ACA to address an economic and social problem that has plagued the Nation for decades: the large number of U.S. residents who are unable or unwilling to obtain health insurance. Whatever one thinks of the policy decision Congress made, it was Congress' prerogative to make it. Reviewed with appropriate deference, the minimum coverage provision, allied to the guaranteed-issue and community-rating prescriptions, should survive measurement under the Commerce and Necessary and Proper Clauses.

■ II

Under the Articles of Confederation, the Constitution's precursor, the regulation of commerce was left to the States. This scheme proved unworkable, because the individual States, understandably focused on their own economic interests, often failed to take actions critical to the success of the Nation as a whole.

The Framers' solution was the Commerce Clause, which, as they perceived it, granted Congress the authority to enact economic legislation "in all Cases for the general Interests of the Union, and also in those Cases to which the States are separately incompetent." *2 Records of the Federal Convention of 1787. . . .*

Consistent with the Framers' intent, we have repeatedly emphasized that Congress's authority under the Commerce Clause is dependent upon "practical" considerations, including "actual experience."

Until today, this Court's pragmatic approach to judging whether Congress validly exercised its commerce power was guided by two familiar principles. First, Congress has the power to regulate economic activities "that substantially affect interstate commerce." *Gonzales v. Raich*, 545 U.S. 1 (2005). This capacious power extends even to local activities that, viewed in the aggregate, have a substantial impact on interstate commerce. When appraising such legislation, we ask only (1) whether Congress had a "rational basis" for concluding that the regulated activity substantially affects interstate commerce, and (2) whether there is a "reasonable connection between the regulatory means selected and the asserted ends."

Straightforward application of these principles would require the Court to hold that the minimum coverage provision is proper Commerce Clause legislation. Beyond dispute, Congress had a rational basis for concluding that the uninsured, as a class, substantially affect interstate commerce. Those without insurance consume billions of dollars of health-care products and services each year. Those goods are produced, sold, and delivered largely by national and regional companies who routinely transact business across state lines. The uninsured also cross state lines to receive care. Some have medical emergencies while away from home. Others, when sick, go to a neighboring State that provides better care for those who have not prepaid for care. . . .

Rather than evaluating the constitutionality of the minimum coverage provision in the manner established by our precedents, The Chief Justice relies on a newly minted constitutional doctrine. The commerce power does not, The Chief Justice announces, permit Congress to "compe[l] individuals to become active in commerce by purchasing a product."

The Chief Justice's novel constraint on Congress' commerce power gains no force from our precedent and for that reason alone warrants disapprobation. But even assuming, for the moment, that Congress lacks authority under the Commerce Clause to "compel individuals not engaged in commerce to purchase

an unwanted product," such a limitation would be inapplicable here. Everyone will, at some point, consume health-care products and services. Thus, if
The Chief Justice is correct that an insurance-purchase requirement can be
applied only to those who "actively" consume health care, the minimum
coverage provision fits the bill. . . .

[The Chief Justice's] argument has multiple flaws. First, more than 60%
of those without insurance visit a hospital or doctor's office each year. Nearly
90% will within five years. . . .

Second, it is Congress's role, not the Court's, to delineate the boundaries
of the market the Legislature seeks to regulate. The Chief Justice defines the
health-care market as including only those transactions that will occur either
in the next instant or within some (unspecified) proximity to the next instant.
But Congress could reasonably have viewed the market from a long-term
perspective, encompassing all transactions virtually certain to occur over the
next decade, not just those occurring here and now.

Third, contrary to The Chief Justice's contention, our precedent does
indeed support "[t]he proposition that Congress may dictate the conduct of
an individual today because of prophesied future activity." In *Wickard*, the
Court upheld a penalty the Federal Government imposed on a farmer who
grew more wheat than he was permitted to grow under the Agricultural
Adjustment Act of 1938 (AAA). He could not be penalized, the farmer
argued, as he was growing the wheat for home consumption, not for sale on
the open market. The Court rejected this argument. Wheat intended for
home consumption, the Court noted, "overhangs the market, and if induced
by rising prices, tends to flow into the market and check price increases
[intended by the AAA]."

Similar reasoning supported the Court's judgment in *Raich*, which upheld
Congress' authority to regulate marijuana grown for personal use. Home-
grown marijuana substantially affects the interstate market for marijuana, we
observed, for "the high demand in the interstate market will [likely] draw
such marijuana into that market."

Our decisions thus acknowledge Congress' authority, under the Commerce Clause, to direct the conduct of an individual today (the farmer in
Wickard, stopped from growing excess wheat; the plaintiff in *Raich*, ordered
to cease cultivating marijuana) because of a prophesied future transaction (the
eventual sale of that wheat or marijuana in the interstate market). Congress'
actions are even more rational in this case, where the future activity (the
consumption of medical care) is certain to occur, the sole uncertainty being
the time the activity will take place. . . .

Failing to learn from this history [of the New Deal Court's decisions],
The Chief Justice plows ahead with his formalistic distinction between those
who are "active in commerce," and those who are not.

It is not hard to show the difficulty courts (and Congress) would encounter in distinguishing statutes that regulate "activity" from those that regulate
"inactivity." *Wickard* is another example. Did the statute there at issue target
activity (the growing of too much wheat) or inactivity (the farmer's failure to
purchase wheat in the marketplace)? If anything, the Court's analysis suggested
the latter. . . .

Underlying The Chief Justice's view that the Commerce Clause must be
confined to the regulation of active participants in a commercial market is a
fear that the commerce power would otherwise know no limits. The joint
dissenters express a similar apprehension. This concern is unfounded.

First, The Chief Justice could certainly uphold the individual mandate without giving Congress *carte blanche* to enact any and all purchase mandates.

Nor would the commerce power be unbridled, absent The Chief Justice's "activity" limitation. Congress would remain unable to regulate non-economic conduct that has only an attenuated effect on interstate commerce and is traditionally left to state law. . . .

As an example of the type of regulation he fears, The Chief Justice cites a Government mandate to purchase green vegetables. One could call this concern "the broccoli horrible." Congress, The Chief Justice posits, might adopt such a mandate, reasoning that an individual's failure to eat a healthy diet, like the failure to purchase health insurance, imposes costs on others. Consider the chain of inferences the Court would have to accept to conclude that a vegetable-purchase mandate was likely to have a substantial effect on the health-care costs borne by lithe Americans. The Court would have to believe that individuals forced to buy vegetables would then eat them (instead of throwing or giving them away), would prepare the vegetables in a healthy way (steamed or raw, not deep-fried), would cut back on unhealthy foods, and would not allow other factors (such as lack of exercise or little sleep) to trump the improved diet. Such "pil[ing of] inference upon inference" is just what the Court refused to do in *Lopez* and *Morrison*. . . .

Supplementing these legal restraints is a formidable check on congressional power: the democratic process. . . .

■ V

Medicaid is a prototypical example of federal-state cooperation in serving the Nation's general welfare. Rather than authorizing a federal agency to administer a uniform national health-care system for the poor, Congress offered States the opportunity to tailor Medicaid grants to their particular needs, so long as they remain within bounds set by federal law. . . .

The Chief Justice acknowledges that Congress may "condition the receipt of [federal] funds on the States' complying with restrictions on the use of those funds," but nevertheless concludes that the 2010 expansion is unduly coercive. His conclusion rests on three premises, each of them essential to his theory. First, the Medicaid expansion is, in The Chief Justice's view, a new grant program, not an addition to the Medicaid program existing before the ACA's enactment. Congress, The Chief Justice maintains, has threatened States with the loss of funds from an old program in an effort to get them to adopt a new one. Second, the expansion was unforeseeable by the States when they first signed on to Medicaid. Third, the threatened loss of funding is so large that the States have no real choice but to participate in the Medicaid expansion. The Chief Justice therefore—for the first time ever—finds an exercise of Congress' spending power unconstitutionally coercive.

Medicaid, as amended by the ACA, however, is not two spending programs; it is a single program with a constant aim—to enable poor persons to receive basic health care when they need it. Given past expansions, plus express statutory warning that Congress may change the requirements participating States must meet, there can be no tenable claim that the ACA fails for lack of notice. Moreover, States have no entitlement to receive any Medicaid funds; they enjoy only the opportunity to accept funds on Congress' terms. Future Congresses are not bound by their predecessors' dispositions; they have authority to spend federal revenue as they see fit. The Federal Government, therefore, is not, as The Chief Justice charges, threatening States with the loss of "existing" funds from one spending program in order to induce them to opt into another program. Congress is simply requiring States to do what States have long been required to do to receive Medicaid funding: comply with the conditions Congress prescribes for participation. . . .

Congress's authority to condition the use of federal funds is not confined to spending programs as first launched. The legislature may, and often does, amend the law, imposing new conditions grant recipients henceforth must meet in order to continue receiving funds. . . .

Congress has broad authority to construct or adjust spending programs to meet its contemporary understanding of "the general Welfare." *Helvering v. Davis,* 301 U.S. 619 (1937). Courts owe a large measure of respect to Congress' characterization of the grant programs it establishes. Even if courts were inclined to second-guess Congress' conception of the character of its legislation, how would reviewing judges divine whether an Act of Congress, purporting to amend a law, is in reality not an amendment, but a new creation? At what point does an extension become so large that it "transforms" the basic law? . . .

The Chief Justice insists that the most recent expansion, in contrast to its predecessors, "accomplishes a shift in kind, not merely degree." But why was Medicaid altered only in degree, not in kind, when Congress required States to cover millions of children and pregnant women? Congress did not "merely alte[r] and expan[d] the boundaries of" the Aid to Families with Dependent Children program. Rather, Congress required participating States to provide coverage tied to the federal poverty level (as it later did in the ACA), rather than to the AFDC program. . . .

When future Spending Clause challenges arrive, as they likely will in the wake of today's decision, how will litigants and judges assess whether "a State has a legitimate choice whether to accept the federal conditions in exchange for federal funds"? Are courts to measure the number of dollars the Federal Government might withhold for noncompliance? The portion of the State's budget at stake? . . .

The coercion inquiry, therefore, appears to involve political judgments that defy judicial calculation.

At bottom, my colleagues' position is that the States' reliance on federal funds limits Congress' authority to alter its spending programs. This gets things backwards: Congress, not the States, is tasked with spending federal money in service of the general welfare. And each successive Congress is empowered to appropriate funds as it sees fit. . . .

For the reasons stated, I agree with The Chief Justice that, as to the validity of the minimum coverage provision, the judgment of the Court of Appeals for the Eleventh Circuit should be reversed. In my view, the provision encounters no constitutional obstruction. Further, I would uphold the Eleventh Circuit's decision that the Medicaid expansion is within Congress' spending power.

☐ *Justice SCALIA, Justice KENNEDY, Justice THOMAS, and Justice ALITO, dissenting.*

The case is easy and straightforward . . . . What is absolutely clear, affirmed by the text of the 1789 Constitution, by the Tenth Amendment ratified in 1791, and by innumerable cases of ours in the 220 years since, is that there are structural limits upon federal power—upon what it can prescribe with respect to private conduct, and upon what it can impose upon the sovereign States.

Whatever may be the conceptual limits upon the Commerce Clause and upon the power to tax and spend, they cannot be such as will enable the Federal Government to regulate all private conduct and to compel the States to function as administrators of federal programs.

That clear principle carries the day here. The striking case of *Wickard v. Filburn*, 317 U.S. 111 (1942), which held that the economic activity of growing wheat, even for one's own consumption, affected commerce sufficiently that it could be regulated, always has been regarded as the *ne plus ultra* of expansive Commerce Clause jurisprudence. To go beyond that, and to say the failure to grow wheat (which is not an economic activity, or any activity at all) nonetheless affects commerce and therefore can be federally regulated, is to make mere breathing in and out the basis for federal prescription and to extend federal power to virtually all human activity.

As for the constitutional power to tax and spend for the general welfare: The Court has long since expanded that beyond (what Madison thought it meant) taxing and spending for those aspects of the general welfare that were within the Federal Government's enumerated powers. Thus, we now have sizable federal Departments devoted to subjects not mentioned among Congress' enumerated powers, and only marginally related to commerce: the Department of Education, the Department of Health and Human Services, the Department of Housing and Urban Development. The principal practical obstacle that prevents Congress from using the tax-and-spend power to assume all the general-welfare responsibilities traditionally exercised by the States is the sheer impossibility of managing a Federal Government large enough to administer such a system. That obstacle can be overcome by granting funds to the States, allowing them to administer the program. That is fair and constitutional enough when the States freely agree to have their powers employed and their employees enlisted in the federal scheme. But it is a blatant violation of the constitutional structure when the States have no choice. . . .

The Court today decides to save a statute Congress did not write. It rules that what the statute declares to be a requirement with a penalty is instead an option subject to a tax. And it changes the intentionally coercive sanction of a total cut-off of Medicaid funds to a supposedly noncoercive cut-off of only the incremental funds that the Act makes available. The Court regards its strained statutory interpretation as judicial modesty. It is not. It amounts instead to a vast judicial overreaching. It creates a debilitated, inoperable version of health-care regulation that Congress did not enact and the public does not expect. It makes enactment of sensible health-care regulation more difficult, since Congress cannot start afresh but must take as its point of departure a jumble of now senseless provisions, provisions that certain interests favored under the Court's new design will struggle to retain. And it leaves the public and the States to expend vast sums of money on requirements that may or may not survive the necessary congressional revision.

The Court's disposition, invented and atextual as it is, does not even have the merit of avoiding constitutional difficulties. It creates them. The holding that the Individual Mandate is a tax raises a difficult constitutional question (what is a direct tax?) that the Court resolves with inadequate deliberation. And the judgment on the Medicaid Expansion issue ushers in new federalism concerns and places an unaccustomed strain upon the Union. Those States that decline the Medicaid Expansion must subsidize, by the federal tax dollars taken from their citizens, vast grants to the States that accept the Medicaid Expansion. If that destabilizing political dynamic, so antagonistic to a harmonious Union, is to be introduced at all, it should be by Congress, not by the Judiciary. The values that should have determined our course today are caution, minimalism, and the understanding that the Federal Government is one of limited powers. But the Court's ruling undermines those values at every turn. In the name of restraint, it overreaches. In the name of constitutional avoidance, it creates new constitutional questions. In the name of cooperative federalism, it undermines state sovereignty. . . .

For the reasons here stated, we would find the Act invalid in its entirety. We respectfully dissent.

☐ *Justice THOMAS, dissenting.*

I dissent for the reasons stated in our joint opinion, but I write separately to say a word about the Commerce Clause. The joint dissent and The Chief Justice correctly apply our precedents to conclude that the Individual Mandate is beyond the power granted to Congress under the Commerce Clause and the Necessary and Proper Clause. Under those precedents, Congress may regulate "economic activity [that] substantially affects interstate commerce." *United States v. Lopez*, 514 U.S. 549 (1995). I adhere to my view that "the very notion of a 'substantial effects' test under the Commerce Clause is inconsistent with the original understanding of Congress' powers and with this Court's early Commerce Clause cases." As I have explained, the Court's continued use of that test "has encouraged the Federal Government to persist in its view that the Commerce Clause has virtually no limits." The Government's unprecedented claim in this suit that it may regulate not only economic activity but also inactivity that substantially affects interstate commerce is a case in point.

7

THE STATES AND
AMERICAN FEDERALISM

A | *States' Power over Commerce and Regulation*

- THE DEVELOPMENT OF LAW

Other Rulings on State Regulatory Powers in Alleged Conflict with Federal Legislation

---

CASE	VOTE	RULING
Bruesewitz v. Wyeth, 131 S.Ct. 1068 (2011)	6:2	Writing for the Court, Justice Scalia held that The National Childhood Vaccine Injury Act,

which created a no-fault program to compensate for vaccine-related injuries, preempts state laws and lawsuits over design-defect claims against vaccine manufacturers. Justices Sotomayor and Ginsburg dissented, and Justice Kagan did not participate.

Williamson v. Mazda Motor of America, 131 S.Ct. 1131 (2011)	8:0	Writing for the Court, Justice Breyer held that The Federal Motor Vehicle Safety Standard 208 does

not preempt state tort suits claiming that manufacturers should have installed lap-and-shoulder seat belts, instead of lap belts, on rear inner seats.

AT&T Mobility v. Concepcion,   5:4   Writing for the majority, Jus-
131 S.Ct. 1741 (2011)   tice Scalia held that California's
                                           "Discover Bank" regulation ran
counter to the purposes of Congress in enacting that legislation and thus was
preempted. Justices Ginsburg, Breyer, Sotomayor, and Kagan dissented.

Chamber of Commerce v.   5:3   Writing for the Court, Chief Jus-
Whiting, 131 S.Ct. 1968   tice Roberts held that the 1986
(2011)   Immigration Reform and Control
                                         Act does not preempt Arizona's
2007 law punishing businesses that hire illegal immigrants by enforcing
"licensing and similar laws," including revoking their licenses. In doing so,
Chief Justice Roberts rejected the argument that immigration was solely the
province of the federal government and signaled that state and local governments may in some cases impose stricter restrictions and sanctions than under
federal law. Justices Breyer, Ginsburg, and Sotomayor dissented, while Justice
Kagan did not participate.

Pliva, Inc. v. Mensing,   5:4   The Federal Drug Administra-
131 S.Ct. 2567 (2011)   tion recently strengthened re-
                                         quirements for warning labels on
prescription drugs—both name-brand and generic—and those regulations
were challenged on the ground that drug manufacturers are also subject to
state tort liability. Writing for the majority, Justice Thomas held that federal
drug regulations requiring name-brand and generic drugs to have the same
warning label preempts state tort law. Because state and federal laws address
label warnings, the federal law is superior, and when it is impossible for a
manufacturer to comply with both state and federal law, the federal law
preempts conflicting state laws. Justices Ginsburg, Breyer, Sotomayor, and
Kagan dissented.

National Meat Association v.   9:0   Writing for the Court, Justice
Harris, 132 S.Ct. 965 (2012)   Kagan held that the Federal Meat
                                         Inspection Act preempts a Califor-
nia law that had barred the processing and sale of nonambulatory pigs inspected
at slaughterhouses.

Kurns v. Railroad Friction   6:3   By a six-to-three vote, the Court
Products, 132 S.Ct. 1261 (2012)   held that the Locomotive Inspec-
                                         tion Act preempts state law design-
defect liability claims for workplace exposure to asbestos.

WOS v. E.M.A., 133 S.Ct.   6:3   Writing for the Court, Justice
1391 (2013)   Kennedy North Carolina's law
                                         requiring up to one-third of any
damages recovered by a Medicaid beneficiary for a tortious injury be paid to
the state for payments it made for medical treatment was preempted by federal
law. Chief Justice Roberts and Justices Scalia and Thomas dissented.

B | *The Tenth and Eleventh Amendments and the States*

In a widely watched case, *Arizona v. United States*, 132 S.Ct. 2492 (2012), involving the federal government's challenge to Arizona's controversial immigration law, the Court struck down three of the four provisions of the law because they were preempted by federal immigration laws under the Supremacy Clause of the Constitution. The majority, though, held that one provision, requiring police to check the immigration status of anyone they detained or arrested, could go into effect but left open the possibility that this provision might be declared unconstitutional if not narrowly applied. Justice Kennedy wrote for the Court, joined by Chief Justice Roberts and Justices Ginsburg, Breyer, and Sotomayor, with Justice Kagan not participating. Chief Justice Roberts's vote was critical, because otherwise the Court would have divided four-to-four and left standing the appellate court's decision striking down all of the law's provisions. Justice Kennedy reaffirmed the federal government's near exclusive authority over immigration matters and on that basis struck down Section 3 of the law, which made it a crime to fail to carry valid immigration papers while in Arizona; Section 5(c), which made it a crime to apply for or hold a job unless one presented valid immigration papers; and Section 6, which would have allowed police to arrest anyone without a warrant if there was probable cause to believe that the individual had done something that would justify deportation. Justices Scalia, Thomas, and Alito dissented from the majority's invalidation of those provisions of Arizona's law.

■ THE DEVELOPMENT OF LAW

Other Recent Rulings on the Tenth Amendment

CASE	VOTE	RULING
Dan's City Used Cars v. Pelkey, 133 S.Ct. 1769 (2013)	9:0	Writing for the Court, Justice Ginsburg held that the Federal Aviation Commission Authorization Act of 1994 preempts state laws "related to a price, route, or service of any motor carrier," but does not preempt state laws pertaining to the storage and disposal of a towed vehicle.
Hillman v. Maretta, 133 S.Ct. 1943 (2013)	9:0	Justice Sotomayor held that the Federal Employees' Group Life Insurance Act of 1954 preempts state laws that conflict with provisions for naming beneficiary of death benefits.

American Trucking Associations v. City of Los Angeles, 133 S.Ct. 2096 (2013) — 9:0 — Justice Kagan held that the Federal Aviation Administration Authorization Act expressly preempts the concession's placard and parking regulation in the Port of Los Angeles.

Arizona v. Inter Tribal Council of Arizona, 133 S.Ct. 476 (2013) — 7:2 — Writing for the Court, Justice Scalia struck down Arizona's law requiring *proof* of citizenship to vote as preempted by the National Voter Registration Act of 1993, which requires only that would-be voters sign a federal form *declaring* that they are citizens. Justice Scalia treated the issue as a statutory question and did not reach the constitutional question of Congress's power over federal elections, but not state elections. Justice Kennedy concurred in part, while Justices Alito and Thomas dissented.

■ THE DEVELOPMENT OF LAW

Other Recent Rulings on the Eleventh Amendment

CASE	VOTE	RULING
Sossamon v. Texas, 131 S.Ct. 1651 (2011)	6:2	While only noting in passing the Eleventh Amendment, Justice Thomas held that state sovereignty, based on precedents and the structure of federalism, immunizes states from suits for monetary damages under the Religious Land Use and Institutionalized Persons Act (RLUIPA). Justices Breyer and Sotomayor dissented, while Justice Kagan took no part in the decision.
Coleman v. Court of Appeals of Maryland, 132 S.Ct. 1327 (2012)	5:4	A bare majority struck down the sick-leave provisions of the Family and Medical Leave Act (FMLA) in holding that Congress had run afoul of the Eleventh Amendment. Writing for the Court, Justice Kennedy distinguished *Nevada Department of Human Resources v. Hibbs,* 538 U.S. 721 (2003) (excerpted in Vol. 1, Ch. 7), which upheld the FMLA's family-care leave provisions on the ground Congress had found evidence of gender discrimination in employers' family-care leave practices and thus had the power under the Fourteenth Amendment to abrogate states' immunity from lawsuits. By contrast, the majority held that Congress failed to establish a connection between gender discrimination and FMLA's sick-leave provisions. Justices Ginsburg, Breyer, Sotomayor, and Kagan dissented.

8

REPRESENTATIVE GOVERNMENT, VOTING RIGHTS, AND ELECTORAL POLITICS

A | *Representative Government and the Franchise*

■ THE DEVELOPMENT OF LAW
Other Rulings Interpreting the Voting Rights Act

CASE	VOTE	RULING
Perry v. Perez, 132 S.Ct. 934 (2012)	9:0	Following the 2010 census Texas received four additional seats in the House of Representatives due

to a 65 percent increase in the Hispanic population. The Republican-controlled legislature redrew district lines that favored the election of Republicans. While that redistricting plan was under the Voting Rights Act's Section Five's preclearance review by the Department of Justice, the plan was challenged and a federal district court redrew the interim maps in order to give Hispanics more opportunities to elect representatives, and which also tended to be more favorable to Democrats. When that plan was challenged, the Supreme Court in a *per curiam* opinion vacated the plan and reprimanded the lower court for not deferring to the state's own policy judgment and redistricting plan.

B | *Voting Rights and the Reapportionment Revolution*

In a brief *per curiam* opinion in *Tennant v. Jefferson County Commission*, 133 S.Ct. 3 (2012), a unanimous Roberts Court upheld a .79 percent population variation in congressional redistricting and emphasized that a redistricting plan does not become unconstitutional just because it could be avoided by "technological advances in redistricting and mapping software." States thus may have some variation in the size of congressional districts, if legislators do so protect incumbents from having to run against each other, to avoid splitting up counties, and to avoid moving many people into a new district from one where they had previously voted. The Court stressed that lower courts should not demand that a state prove specifically how each of those goals would be satisfied by not adopting precisely equally populated ("zero variance") districts.

In a major ruling in *Shelby County, Alabama v. Holder*, 133 S.Ct. 2612 (2013), a bare majority invalidated Section 4 of the Voting Rights Act of 1965 that specifies a formula for signaling out (based on discriminatory tests and low voter registration and turnout) certain states and counties for preclearance review by the Department of Justice (DoJ) under Section 5 of the law. In order to ensure against the dilution of minorities' voting rights, the law required DoJ preclearance of any changes in election laws in Alabama, Georgia, Louisiana, Mississippi, South Carolina, Texas, and Virginia as well as in Alaska, Arizona, and parts of several other states. That provision continued when Congress renewed the Voting Rights Act in 2006 for another 25 years. But Chief Justice Roberts held that times have changed and that Congress must revise the formula (and, if not, the DoJ must independently pursue attempts to dilute the voting power of minorities through changes in election laws). He dismissed the continued use of a formula based on "40-year-old facts," when the country had changed and more African Americans voted and were elected to office than they had been 50 years ago. In his words: "Congress could have updated the coverage formula [in 2006] but did not do so. . . . Its failure to act leaves us today with no choice but to declare [Section 4] unconstitutional. . . . Our country has changed, and while any racial discrimination in voting is too much, Congress must ensure that the legislation it passes to remedy that problem speaks to current conditions." In dissent, Justice Ginsburg, joined by Justices Breyer, Sotomayor, and Kagan, countered that the majority misread the country's history of racial progress and inserted itself into a role reserved for Congress. As she put it: "When confronting the most constitutionally invidious form of discrimination, and the most fundamental right in our democratic system, Congress's power to act is at its height."

C | *Campaigns and Elections*

The Roberts Court revisited the controversy over public financing of campaigns for public office in *Arizona Free Enterprise Club's Freedom Club PAC v. Bennett* (2011) (excerpted below). In *Buckley v. Valeo*, 424 U.S. 1 (1976) (excerpted in Vol. 1, Ch. 8), the Burger Court upheld the transfer of taxpayer contributions (through a tax return checkoff) to presidential candidates willing to accept campaign spending limits in exchange for receiving public funding. In doing so, the Court reasoned that Congress had created a system "to reduce the deleterious influence of large contributions on our political process, to facilitate communication by candidates with the electorate, and to free candidates from the rigors of fund-raising." In *Davis v. Federal Election Commission*, 554 U.S. 724 (2008), however, the Roberts Court signaled a different predisposition. Although *Davis* did not involve public funding per se, but rather self-financed candidates, it considered the effects of candidates spending their own money. A bare majority struck down the so-called "millionaire's amendment," imposing limits on candidates' personal expenditures, to the Bipartisan Campaign Reform Act of 2002 (also known as "the McCain-Feingold law"). Notably, a bare majority of the Rehnquist Court invalidated other provisions of that law in *McConnell v. Federal Election Commission*, 540 U.S. 93 (2003) (excerpted in Vol. 1, Ch. 8), as did a bare majority of the Roberts Court when striking down its provisions forbidding corporations and unions from using general funds for direct contributions to candidates for certain federal offices, in *Citizens United v. Federal Election Commission*, 130 S.Ct. 876 (2010) (excerpted in Vol. 1, Ch. 8).

Writing for the Court in *Davis*, Justice Alito held that the provision effectively imposed different contribution limits on competing candidates. Hence, Congress (not the voters) would determine whom to favor in an election and the differing restrictions put "a drag" on self-financed candidates' free speech. At issue in *Arizona Free Enterprise Club's Freedom Club*

PAC v. Bennett (excerpted below) was Arizona's law providing public subsidies for candidates who accept in exchange limits on campaign contributions and who would receive an additional subsidy if their self-financed opponent spent more than the state limits on campaign spending; in no event would self-financed candidates receive public funding.

A bare majority of the Roberts Court also reaffirmed its controversial ruling in *Citizens United* in a one-page *per curiam* opinion in *American Tradition Partnership v. Bullock*, 132 S.Ct. 1307 (2012). In a summary (without briefing and oral arguments), the majority struck down a 100-year-old Montana law that banned corporations in state elections from spending any money to support or oppose a candidate or political party. In doing so, it overruled the state supreme court's decision upholding the law, in spite of *Citizens United*; the state had a history of corruption that justified the law. Justice Breyer, joined by Justices Ginsburg, Sotomayor, and Kagan, dissented and would have granted *certiorari* and reconsidered the decision in *Citizens United*.

In *Arizona v. Inter Tribal Council of Arizona*, 133 S.Ct. 476 (2013), however, the Court struck down Arizona's law requiring proof of citizenship to vote as inconsistent with the National Voter Registration Act of 1993, which requires only that would-be voters sign a federal form declaring that they are citizens. Writing for the Court, Justice Scalia treated the issue as a statutory question and did not reach the constitutional question of Congress's power over federal elections but not state elections. Somewhat confusingly Justice Scalia indicated that a state could ask for exemptions from the law for their regulations and, if denied by the federal government, sue and pursue a constitutional change. Justice Kennedy concurred in part, while Justices Alito and Thomas dissented.

Arizona Free Enterprise Club's Freedom Club PAC v. Bennett

131 S.Ct. 2806 (2011)

The constitutionality of Arizona's Clean Elections Act of 1998, which created a system of public campaign financing that subsidizes candidates for office, was challenged by several past and future candidates for office and political action committees. The law was adopted in a statewide initiative by a 51 to 49 percent margin, amid scandals over campaign financing that lead to the criminal prosecution of two governors and a number of state legislators. It created a subsidy scheme for races for governor, lieutenant governor, attorney general, state legislators, among other elected offices, and created a Citizens Clean Elections Commission to enforce the law. Under the statute, candidates may obtain public subsidies, though they may not pay for their campaigns entirely with public funds. They qualify for a subsidy if they raise a specified amount in private donations, provided that each contribution is no more than five dollars, and if their campaigns spend no more than the limits set by state law. Once they receive a subsidy they may no longer raise private funds and are limited to spending only the amount of the subsidy. However, there is also a "matching funds" provision, which was the focus of the challenge to the law. If a subsidized candidate has a "self-financed" opponent—who spends his or her own money or raises it from private contributions or political action committees—and spends more than the initial subsidy, then the subsidized candidate may receive an additional subsidy (but no more than twice the amount of the initial subsidy, and with 6 percent of the additional subsidy deducted to cover expenses). Moreover, if an independent group supports the subsidized candidate, the self-financed candidate receives no public funding. When the law went into effect in 2000, the matching-funds provision was challenged by several past and future would-be self-financed candidates and two political action committees that planned to support such candidates. A federal district court struck down the provision as a violation of the First Amendment. The Court of Appeals for the Ninth Circuit in turn reversed and upheld the matching-funds provision, upon concluding that the burden on self-financed candidates was minimal. Although the provision went into effect, challengers persuaded the Supreme Court to block the appellate court's decision upholding the provision in a June 2010 order. The challengers then filed petitions to the Court, which granted review.

The appellate court's decision was reversed. Chief Justice Roberts delivered the opinion for the Court. Justice Kagan filed a dissent, which Justices Ginsburg, Breyer, and Sotomayor joined.

□ *CHIEF JUSTICE ROBERTS delivered the opinion of the Court.*

"Discussion of public issues and debate on the qualifications of candidates are integral to the operation" of our system of government. *Buckley v. Valeo*, 424 U.S. 1 (1976). As a result, the First Amendment "'has its fullest and most urgent application' to speech uttered during a campaign for political office." *Eu v. San Francisco County Democratic Central Comm.*, 489 U.S. 214 (1989). "Laws that burden political speech are" accordingly "subject to strict scrutiny, which requires the Government to prove that the restriction furthers a compelling interest and is narrowly tailored to achieve that interest." *Citizens United v. Federal Election Comm'n*, [130 S.Ct. 876] (2010).

Applying these principles, we have invalidated government-imposed restrictions on campaign expenditures, *Buckley*, restraints on independent expenditures applied to express advocacy groups, [*Federal Election Commission v.*]

Massachusetts Citizens for Life [479 U.S. 238 (1986)], limits on uncoordinated political party expenditures, *Colorado Republican Federal Campaign Comm. v. Federal Election Comm'n*, 518 U.S. 604 (1996) (*Colorado I*), and regulations barring unions, nonprofit and other associations, and corporations from making independent expenditures for electioneering communication, *Citizens United.*

At the same time, we have subjected strictures on campaign-related speech that we have found less onerous to a lower level of scrutiny and upheld those restrictions. For example, after finding that the restriction at issue was "closely drawn" to serve a "sufficiently important interest," see, e.g., *McConnell v. Federal Election Comm'n*, 540 U.S. 93 (2003); *Nixon v. Shrink Missouri Government PA*, 528 U.S. 377 (2000), we have upheld government-imposed limits on contributions to candidates, *Buckley*, caps on coordinated party expenditures, *Federal Election Comm'n v. Colorado Republican Federal Campaign Comm.*, 533 U.S. 431 (2001) (*Colorado II*), and requirements that political funding sources disclose their identities, *Citizens United.*

Although the speech of the candidates and independent expenditure groups that brought this suit is not directly capped by Arizona's matching funds provision, those parties contend that their political speech is substantially burdened by the state law in the same way that speech was burdened by the law we recently found invalid in *Davis v. Federal Election Comm'n*, 554 U.S. 724 (2008). In *Davis*, we considered a First Amendment challenge to the so-called "Millionaire's Amendment" of the Bipartisan Campaign Reform Act of 2002. Under that Amendment, if a candidate for the United States House of Representatives spent more than $350,000 of his personal funds, "a new, asymmetrical regulatory scheme [came] into play." The opponent of the candidate who exceeded that limit was permitted to collect individual contributions up to $6,900 per contributor—three times the normal contribution limit of $2,300. The candidate who spent more than the personal funds limit remained subject to the original contribution cap. Davis argued that this scheme "burden[ed] his exercise of his First Amendment right to make unlimited expenditures of his personal funds because" doing so had "the effect of enabling his opponent to raise more money and to use that money to finance speech that counteract[ed] and thus diminishe[d] the effectiveness of Davis' own speech."

In addressing the constitutionality of the Millionaire's Amendment, we acknowledged that the provision did not impose an outright cap on a candidate's personal expenditures. We nonetheless concluded that the Amendment was unconstitutional because it forced a candidate "to choose between the First Amendment right to engage in unfettered political speech and subjection to discriminatory fundraising limitations." Any candidate who chose to spend more than $350,000 of his own money was forced to "shoulder a special and potentially significant burden" because that choice gave fundraising advantages to the candidate's adversary. We determined that this constituted an "unprecedented penalty" and "impose[d] a substantial burden on the exercise of the First Amendment right to use personal funds for campaign speech," and concluded that the Government had failed to advance any compelling interest that would justify such a burden.

The logic of *Davis* largely controls our approach to this case. Much like the burden placed on speech in *Davis*, the matching funds provision "imposes an unprecedented penalty on any candidate who robustly exercises [his] First Amendment right[s]."

Once a privately financed candidate has raised or spent more than the State's initial grant to a publicly financed candidate, each personal dollar spent by the privately financed candidate results in an award of almost one additional dollar to his opponent. That plainly forces the privately financed candidate to "shoulder a special and potentially significant burden" when choosing to exercise his First Amendment right to spend funds on behalf of his candidacy. If the law at issue in *Davis* imposed a burden on candidate speech, the Arizona law unquestionably does so as well.

The penalty imposed by Arizona's matching funds provision is different in some respects from the penalty imposed by the law we struck down in *Davis*. But those differences make the Arizona law more constitutionally problematic, not less. First, the penalty in *Davis* consisted of raising the contribution limits for one of the candidates. The candidate who benefited from the increased limits still had to go out and raise the funds. . . Here the benefit to the publicly financed candidate is the direct and automatic release of public money. That is a far heavier burden than in *Davis*.

Second, depending on the specifics of the election at issue, the matching funds provision can create a multiplier effect. [I]f the spending cap were exceeded, each dollar spent by the privately funded candidate would result in an additional dollar of campaign funding to each of that candidate's [multiple] publicly financed opponents. In such a situation, the matching funds provision forces privately funded candidates to fight a political hydra of sorts. . . .

Third, unlike the law at issue in *Davis*, all of this is to some extent out of the privately financed candidate's hands. Even if that candidate opted to spend less than the initial public financing cap, any spending by independent expenditure groups to promote the privately financed candidate's election—regardless whether such support was welcome or helpful—could trigger matching funds. . . .

The burdens that this regime places on independent expenditure groups are akin to those imposed on the privately financed candidates themselves. Just as with the candidate the independent group supports, the more money spent on that candidate's behalf or in opposition to a publicly funded candidate, the more money the publicly funded candidate receives from the State. And just as with the privately financed candidate, the effect of a dollar spent on election speech is a guaranteed financial payout to the publicly funded candidate the group opposes. Moreover, spending one dollar can result in the flow of dollars to multiple candidates the group disapproves of, dollars directly controlled by the publicly funded candidate or candidates. . . .

We have repeatedly rejected the argument that the government has a compelling state interest in "leveling the playing field" that can justify undue burdens on political speech. *Citizens United*. In *Davis*, we stated that discriminatory contribution limits meant to "level electoral opportunities for candidates of different personal wealth" did not serve "a legitimate government objective," let alone a compelling one. And in *Buckley*, we held that limits on overall campaign expenditures could not be justified by a purported government "interest in equalizing the financial resources of candidates." . . .

We do not today call into question the wisdom of public financing as a means of funding political candidacy. That is not our business. But determining whether laws governing campaign finance violate the First Amendment is very much our business. In carrying out that responsibility over the past 35 years, we have upheld some restrictions on speech and struck down others.

We have said that governments "may engage in public financing of election campaigns" and that doing so can further "significant governmental interest[s]," such as the state interest in preventing corruption. *Buckley.* But the goal of creating a viable public financing scheme can only be pursued in a manner consistent with the First Amendment. . . .

The judgment of the Court of Appeals for the Ninth Circuit is reversed.

☐ *Justice KAGAN, with whom Justice GINSBURG, Justice BREYER, and Justice SOTOMAYOR join, dissenting.*

Imagine two States, each plagued by a corrupt political system. In both States, candidates for public office accept large campaign contributions in exchange for the promise that, after assuming office, they will rank the donors' interests ahead of all others. As a result of these bargains, politicians ignore the public interest, sound public policy languishes, and the citizens lose confidence in their government.

Recognizing the cancerous effect of this corruption, voters of the first State, acting through referendum, enact several campaign finance measures previously approved by this Court. They cap campaign contributions; require disclosure of substantial donations; and create an optional public financing program that gives candidates a fixed public subsidy if they refrain from private fundraising. But these measures do not work. Individuals who "bundle" campaign contributions become indispensable to candidates in need of money. Simple disclosure fails to prevent shady dealing. And candidates choose not to participate in the public financing system because the sums provided do not make them competitive with their privately financed opponents. So the State remains afflicted with corruption.

Voters of the second State, having witnessed this failure, take an ever-so-slightly different tack to cleaning up their political system. They too enact contribution limits and disclosure requirements. But they believe that the greatest hope of eliminating corruption lies in creating an effective public financing program, which will break candidates' dependence on large donors and bundlers. These voters realize, based on the first State's experience, that such a program will not work unless candidates agree to participate in it. And candidates will participate only if they know that they will receive sufficient funding to run competitive races. So the voters enact a program that carefully adjusts the money given to would-be officeholders, through the use of a matching funds mechanism, in order to provide this assurance. The program does not discriminate against any candidate or point of view, and it does not restrict any person's ability to speak. In fact, by providing resources to many candidates, the program creates more speech and thereby broadens public debate. And just as the voters had hoped, the program accomplishes its mission of restoring integrity to the political system. The second State rids itself of corruption.

A person familiar with our country's core values—our devotion to democratic self-governance, as well as to "uninhibited, robust, and wide-open" debate, *New York Times Co. v. Sullivan*, 376 U.S. 254 (1964)—might expect this

Court to celebrate, or at least not to interfere with, the second State's success. But today, the majority holds that the second State's system—the system that produces honest government, working on behalf of all the people—clashes with our Constitution. The First Amendment, the majority insists, requires us all to rely on the measures employed in the first State, even when they have failed to break the stranglehold of special interests on elected officials.

I disagree. The First Amendment's core purpose is to foster a healthy, vibrant political system full of robust discussion and debate. Nothing in Arizona's anti-corruption statute, the Arizona Citizens Clean Elections Act, violates this constitutional protection. To the contrary, the Act promotes the values underlying both the First Amendment and our entire Constitution by enhancing the "opportunity for free political discussion to the end that government may be responsive to the will of the people." I therefore respectfully dissent.

Campaign finance reform over the last century has focused on one key question: how to prevent massive pools of private money from corrupting our political system. If an officeholder owes his election to wealthy contributors, he may act for their benefit alone, rather than on behalf of all the people. As we recognized in *Buckley v. Valeo*, our seminal campaign finance case, large private contributions may result in "political quid pro quo[s]," which undermine the integrity of our democracy. And even if these contributions are not converted into corrupt bargains, they still may weaken confidence in our political system because the public perceives "the opportunities for abuse[s]." To prevent both corruption and the appearance of corruption—and so to protect our democratic system of governance—citizens have implemented reforms designed to curb the power of special interests.

Among these measures, public financing of elections has emerged as a potentially potent mechanism to preserve elected officials' independence. President Theodore Roosevelt proposed the reform as early as 1907 in his State of the Union address. "The need for collecting large campaign funds would vanish," he said, if the government "provided an appropriation for the proper and legitimate expenses" of running a campaign, on the condition that a "party receiving campaign funds from the Treasury" would forgo private fundraising. The idea was—and remains—straightforward. Candidates who rely on public, rather than private, moneys are "beholden [to] no person and, if elected, should feel no post-election obligation toward any contributor." By supplanting private cash in elections, public financing eliminates the source of political corruption.

For this reason, public financing systems today dot the national landscape. Almost one-third of the States have adopted some form of public financing, and so too has the Federal Government for presidential elections. . . . We declared the presidential public financing system constitutional in *Buckley v. Valeo*. . . .

But this model, which distributes a lump-sum grant at the beginning of an election cycle, has a significant weakness: It lacks a mechanism for setting the subsidy at a level that will give candidates sufficient incentive to participate, while also conserving public resources. Public financing can achieve its goals only if a meaningful number of candidates receive the state subsidy, rather than raise private funds. But a public funding program must be voluntary to pass constitutional muster, because of its restrictions on contributions and expenditures. And candidates will choose to sign up only if the subsidy provided enables them to run competitive races. If the grant is pegged too low, it puts the participating candidate at a disadvantage: Because he has agreed to spend no more than the amount of the subsidy, he will lack the means to respond if his privately funded opponent spends over that threshold. So when lump-sum grants do not keep up with campaign expenditures, more and more candidates will choose not to participate. But if the subsidy is set too high, it may impose an unsustainable burden on the public fisc. At the least, hefty grants will waste public resources in the many state races where lack of competition makes such funding unnecessary.

The difficulty, then, is in finding the Goldilocks solution—not too large, not too small, but just right. And this in a world of countless variables—where the amount of money needed to run a viable campaign against a privately funded candidate depends on, among other things, the district, the office, and the election cycle. A state may set lump-sum grants district-by-district, based on spending in past elections; but even that approach leaves out many factors—including the resources of the privately funded candidate—that alter the competitiveness of a seat from one election to the next. In short, the dynamic nature of our electoral system makes *ex ante* predictions about campaign expenditures almost impossible. And that creates a chronic problem for lump-sum public financing programs, because inaccurate estimates produce subsidies that either dissuade candidates from participating or waste taxpayer money. And so States have made adjustments to the lump-sum scheme that we approved in *Buckley*, in attempts to more effectively reduce corruption.

The hallmark of Arizona's program is its inventive approach to the challenge that bedevils all public financing schemes: fixing the amount of the subsidy. For each electoral contest, the system calibrates the size of the grant automatically to provide sufficient—but no more than sufficient—funds to induce voluntary participation. In effect, the program's designers found the Goldilocks solution, which produces the "just right" grant to ensure that a participant in the system has the funds needed to run a competitive race. . . .

The question here is whether this modest adjustment to the public financing program that we approved in *Buckley* makes the Arizona law unconstitutional. The majority contends that the matching funds provision "substantially burdens protected political speech" and does not "serv[e] a compelling state interest." But the Court is wrong on both counts.

Arizona's statute does not impose a "restriction," or "substantia[l] burde[n]," on expression. The law has quite the opposite effect: It subsidizes and so produces more political speech. We recognized in *Buckley* that, for this reason, public financing of elections "facilitate[s] and enlarge[s] public discussion," in support of First Amendment values. And what we said then is just as true today. Except in a world gone topsy-turvy, additional campaign speech and electoral competition is not a First Amendment injury.

At every turn, the majority tries to convey the impression that Arizona's matching fund statute is of a piece with laws prohibiting electoral speech. The majority invokes the language of "limits," "bar[s]," and "restraints." . . .

There is just one problem. Arizona's matching funds provision does not restrict, but instead subsidizes, speech. . . .

And under the First Amendment, that makes all the difference. In case after case, year upon year, we have distinguished between speech restrictions and speech subsidies. "'There is a basic difference,'" we have held, "'between direct state interference with [First Amendment] protected activity and state encouragement'" of other expression. *Rust v. Sullivan*, 500 U.S. 173 (1991). That is because subsidies, by definition and contra the majority, do not restrict any speech.

No one can claim that Arizona's law discriminates against particular ideas, and so violates the First Amendment's sole limitation on speech subsidies. The State throws open the doors of its public financing program to all candidates who meet minimal eligibility requirements and agree not to raise private funds. . . .

Most important, and as just suggested, the very notion that additional speech constitutes a "burden" is odd and unsettling. Here is a simple fact: Arizona imposes nothing remotely resembling a coercive penalty on privately funded candidates. The State does not jail them, fine them, or subject them to any kind of lesser disability. The only "burden" in this case comes from the grant of a subsidy to another person, and the opportunity that subsidy allows for responsive speech. . . .

But put to one side this most fundamental objection to the majority's argument; even then, has the majority shown that the burden resulting from the Arizona statute is "substantial"? I will not quarrel with the majority's assertion that responsive speech by one candidate may make another candidate's speech less effective; that, after all, is the whole idea of the First Amendment, and a benefit of having more responsive speech. And I will assume that the operation of this statute may on occasion deter a privately funded candidate from spending money, and conveying ideas by that means. . . . Still, does that effect count as a severe burden on expression? By the measure of our prior decisions—which have upheld campaign reforms with an equal or greater impact on speech—the answer is no.

Number one: Any system of public financing, including the lump-sum model upheld in *Buckley* imposes a similar burden on privately funded candidates. . . .

Number two: Our decisions about disclosure and disclaimer requirements show the Court is wrong. Starting in *Buckley* and continuing through last Term, the Court has repeatedly declined to view these requirements as a substantial First Amendment burden, even though they discourage some campaign speech. . . . And much more recently, in *Citizens United* and *Doe v. Reed*, [130 S.Ct. 486] (2010), we followed that precedent. "Disclosure requirements may burden the ability to speak," we reasoned, but they "do not prevent anyone from speaking." So too here. Like a disclosure rule, the matching funds provision may occasionally deter, but "impose[s] no ceiling" on electoral expression. . . .

For all these reasons, the Court errs in holding that the government action in this case substantially burdens speech and so requires the State to offer a compelling interest. But in any event, Arizona has come forward with just such an interest, explaining that the Clean Elections Act attacks corruption and the appearance of corruption in the State's political system. The majority's denigration of this interest—the suggestion that it either is not real or does not matter—wrongly prevents Arizona from protecting the strength and integrity of its democracy. . . .

■ THE DEVELOPMENT OF LAW

Other Rulings on Campaigns and Elections

CASE	VOTE	RULING
Nevada Commission on Ethics v. Carrington, 131 S.Ct. 857 (2011)	9:0	Nevada's Ethics in Government Law requires public officials to recuse themselves "from voting on, or advocating the passage or

failure of 'a matter with respect to which the independence of judgment of a reasonable person in his situation would be materially affected by' ... '[h]is commitment in a private capacity to the interests of others.'" The commission investigated an elected local official, who had voted to approve a hotel/casino project proposed by a company that used his longtime friend and campaign manager as a paid consultant, and concluded he should have recused himself and therefore censured him. The official challenged that decision and the state supreme court held that the law was overly broad and ran afoul of the First Amendment. Writing for the Court, Justice Scalia reversed and held that the law was not unconstitutional but a "reasonable time, place, and manner" limitation.

Arizona v. Inter Tribal Council of Arizona, 133 S.Ct. 476 (2013)	7:2	Writing for the Court, Justice Scalia struck down Arizona's law requiring *proof* of citizenship to vote as inconsistent with the

National Voter Registration Act of 1993, which requires only that would-be voters sign a federal form *declaring* that they are citizens. Justice Scalia treated the issue as a statutory question and did not reach the constitutional question of Congress's power over federal elections but not state elections. Justice Kennedy concurred in part, while Justices Alito and Thomas dissented.

9

ECONOMIC RIGHTS AND AMERICAN CAPITALISM

■ THE DEVELOPMENT OF LAW

Other Rulings on the Takings Clause

CASE	VOTE	RULING
Arkansas Game and Fish Commission v. United States, 133 S.Ct. 1856 (2012)	8:0	Writing for a unanimous Court, with Justice Kagan recused, Justice Ginsburg held that the temporary flooding, caused by the U.S. Army

Corp of Engineers between 1993 and 2000 that destroyed nearly 18 million board feet of timber, was not excluded from Takings Clause liability and that "government-induced ? of limited duration may be compensable" under the Fifth Amendment. Justice Ginsburg held that temporary invasions of property are subject to a balancing test to determine they constitute a takings and outlined several factors to be considered, including the duration of the invasion, whether the invasion was intentional, the characteristics of the law, and the property owner's "reasonable investment-backed expectations."

Koontz v. St. Johns River Water Management District, 133 S.Ct. 2586 (2013)	5:4	Writing for the Court, Justice Alito held that the government may not place permit conditions that require landowners to give up

property rights unless there is a "nexus" and "rough proportionality" between the condition and the effects of land use. Extortionate governmental demands run afoul of the Fifth Amendment right to just compensation and the unconstitutional conditions doctrine prohibits them, as set forth in *Nollan v. California Coastal Commission*, 483 U.S. 825 (1987) and *Dollan v. City of Tigard*, 512 U.S. 374 (1994). Here, Florida required landowners to acquire building permits in order to build near wetlands and as a condition provide public easement as well as spend money to develop public lands elsewhere in the state. Koontz refused and the state denied his building permit. Justice Alito held that the *Nollan/Dollan* standard applies as a basis for challenging the denial (not just to the approval) of a building permit based on the Fifth Amendment Takings Clause. Justices Ginsbug, Breyer, Sotomayor, and Kagan dissented.

SUPREME COURT WATCH 2013
VOLUME TWO

4

THE NATIONALIZATION
OF THE
BILL OF RIGHTS

B | *The Rise and (Partial) Retreat of the "Due Process Revolution"*

■ THE DEVELOPMENT OF LAW

Other Recent Rulings on Substantive and Procedural Due Process

CASE	VOTE	RULING
District Attorney's Office for Third Judicial District v. Osborne, 129 S.Ct. 2308 (2009)	5:4	Writing for the Court, Chief Justice Roberts rejected a *substantive due process* claim to file a Section 1983 lawsuit against state officials

for violating a constitutional right of access to the result of DNA testing that was used as evidence at trial. In doing so, the chief justice emphasized that states were developing their own standards for the introduction and access to DNA evidence and that there was no need to constitutionalize the matter. Justices Stevens, Souter, Ginsburg, and Breyer dissented.

Skinner v. Switzer, 131 S.Ct. 1289 (2011) — 6:3

Distinguishing the ruling in *District Attorney's Office v. Osborne,* 129 S.Ct. 2308 (2009), the Court held that Texas's denial of all DNA evidence, specifically unused evidence at trial, to a death-row inmate violated procedural due process and thus permitted Section 1983 civil rights suits. Writing for the Court, Justice Ginsburg emphasized the narrowness of the holding and that it leaves "slim room" to bring such challenges. The dissenters—Justices Kennedy, Thomas, and Alito—protested that the ruling provided a "roadmap" for state inmates to reopen DNA-access claims after having lost in *habeas corpus* appeals, and therefore opened the "floodgate" for such lawsuits.

Turner v. Rogers, 131 S.Ct. 2507 (2011) — 5:4

Writing for the Court, Justice Breyer held that due process does not require states to provide attorneys for indigents in civil proceedings, even if they may result in incarceration for willful contempt in repeatedly failing to make child-support payments. However, the majority ruled that in such proceedings states should provide "substitute procedural safeguards," such as (1) notice to the defendant that his ability to pay is a critical issue in contempt proceedings; (2) the use of a form to elicit relevant financial information; (3) an opportunity at the hearing to respond to statements and questions about financial status; and (4) an express finding by the court that the defendant has the ability to pay. Chief Justice Roberts and Justices Scalia, Thomas, and Alito dissented.

FCC v. Fox Television Stations, Inc., 132 S.Ct. 2307 (2012) — 8:0

Writing for the Court, Justice Kennedy held that the Federal Communications Commission violated the Due Process Clause when it sanctioned broadcasters for "fleeting indecent" broadcasts without providing them with fair notice of the Commission's change in policy regarding "fleeting expletives" on the airwaves. Justice Sotomayor did not participate in the decision. It thus avoided the constitutional challenge.

5

FREEDOM OF EXPRESSION
AND ASSOCIATION

Notably, the Court upheld, over First Amendment objections, Congress' power under the Copyright Clause to extend copyright protection to millions of books, films, and musical compositions by foreign writers and artists that were once in the public domain. In 1994, Congress enacted a law to implement a global trade agreement on intellectual property. The constitutionality of that law was challenged as a violation of the First Amendment right of a group of orchestra conductors, educators, performers, and producers who had previously had access to and reproduced creative works whose copyright protection had expired. Writing for the Court in *Golan v. Holder*, 132 S.Ct. 873 (2012), Justice Ginsburg rejected the First Amendment challenge as inconsistent with historical and international practices, as well as dismissed the claim that royalties for using such works would now be prohibitive for many scholars and production companies. Justice Kagan recused herself, while Justices Breyer and Alito dissented.

A | *Judicial Approaches to the First Amendment*

(2) *Judicial Line Drawing:* Ad hoc *and Definitional Balancing*

A majority of the Roberts Court continued in a series of decisions to defend the First Amendment guarantee for freedom of expression and to refuse to carve out exceptions or create new categories of unprotected speech. In *United States v. Alvarez*, 132 S.Ct. 2537 (2012), a plurality declared unconstitutional the Stolen Valor Act, which had made it a crime to lie about receiving a military decoration or medal, punishable by up to a year in prison. Writing for the Court, Justice Kennedy held that the government had "not demonstrated that false statements generally should constitute a new category of unprotected speech." Underscoring its defense of the First Amendment, Justice Kennedy continued: "The remedy for speech that is false is speech that is true. This is the ordinary course in a free society. The response to the unreasoned is the rational; to the uninformed, the enlightened; to the straight-out lie, the simple truth. . . . The First Amendment itself ensures the right to respond to speech we do not like, and for good reason. Freedom of speech and thought flows not from the beneficence of the state but from the inalienable rights of the person."

By a seven-to-two vote in *Brown v. Entertainment Merchants Association* (excerpted below), the Court also struck down California's law punishing the sales of violent video games to minors. Justice Scalia's opinion for the Court swept broadly in reaffirming the broad protection of the First Amendment and refusing to carve out another category of unprotected speech. Justice Alito, joined by Chief Justice Roberts, concurred but left open the possibility of upholding such a law if properly framed. Justices Thomas and Breyer dissented. Notably, Justice Thomas would have upheld the law based on the "original understanding" of freedom of speech, while Justice Breyer would have done so based on social science data and the projected consequences of violent video games.

In addition, the justices continued to grapple with the problem of defining the scope of freedom of expression with respect to government-funded speech, in *Agency for International Development v. Alliance for Open Society International, Inc.*, 133 S.Ct. 2321 (2013). Writing for the majority, Chief Justice Roberts ruled that government runs afoul of the First Amendment when it requires as a condition of receiving federal funds that recipients publicly endorse its policies. In 2003 Congress enacted the United States Leadership Against HIV/AIDS, Tuberculosis, and Malaria Act, establishing a broad range of programs and appropriating billions of dollars for nongovernmental organizations to combat HIV/AIDS worldwide. The law also imposed two conditions: (1) No funds could be used to advocate the legalization of prostitution and (2) no funds could be awarded unless an organization had "a policy explicitly opposing prostitution." A number of organizations challenged the constitutionality of the latter requirement. They did not advocate prostitution but wanted to remain neutral because otherwise their efforts to educate prostitutes about the spread of HIV/AIDS might be hindered, and hence claimed that the requirement violated their freedom of speech. A majority of the Court agreed and distinguished *Rust v. Sullivan*, 500 U.S. 173 (1991) (excerpted in Vol. 2, Ch. 5), from *Agency for International Development*. *Rust* held that Congress's denial of federal funds for the purpose of advocating abortion did not violate the First Amendment. That was acceptable, Chief Justice Roberts reasoned, because Congress may impose conditions on how its appropriations are spent, and organizations receiving funding could still use private funds for their advocacy. In *Agency for International Development*, however, Congress compelled the advocacy of a particular message as a condition for receiving funding. And the First Amendment forbids government from dictating what people may say. As the chief justice put it: "By requiring recipients to profess a specific belief, the [command of what people say] goes beyond defining the limits of the federally funded program to defining the recipient." Justice Scalia, joined by Justice Thomas, dissented.

Brown v. Entertainment Merchants Association
131 S.Ct. 2729 (2011)

In 2005, California enacted a law requiring the labeling of video games containing violence and the sales of such videos to minors, with up to $1,000 for violations. When the constitutionality of the law was challenged, the state argued for the extension of a constitutional standard, created for cases involving the protection of minors from obscene materials, to violent materials, rather than obscenity. That standard derives from *Ginsberg v. New York*, 390 U.S. 629 (1968). The statute defines a violent video game as one depicting the "killing, maiming, dismembering, or sexually assaulting the image of a human being" in a manner that a reasonable person would find appeals to "a deviant or morbid interest" of minors, and is "patently offensive" to prevailing standards of what is suitable for minors and causes the game—as a whole—to lack "serious, artistic, political or scientific value" for minors. The Court of Appeals for the Ninth Circuit found the statute to run afoul of the First Amendment, rejecting the proposed extension of the *Ginsberg* standard and using instead the "strict scrutiny" test. It held that there was no proof that playing such games harms, physically or psychologically, minors. The state appealed and the Court granted review.

The appellate court's ruling was affirmed by a seven-to-two vote. Justice Scalia delivered the opinion for the Court. Justice Alito filed a concurrence, joined by Chief Justice Roberts. Justices Thomas and Breyer each issued dissenting opinions.

☐ *Justice SCALIA delivered the opinion of the Court.*

Like the protected books, plays, and movies that preceded them, video games communicate ideas—and even social messages—through many familiar literary devices (such as characters, dialogue, plot, and music) and through features distinctive to the medium (such as the player's interaction with the virtual world). That suffices to confer First Amendment protection. . . . And whatever the challenges of applying the Constitution to ever-advancing technology, "the basic principles of freedom of speech and the press, like the First Amendment's command, do not vary" when a new and different medium for communication appears. *Joseph Burstyn, Inc. v. Wilson*, 343 U.S. 495 (1952).

The most basic of those principles is this: "[A]s a general matter, . . . government has no power to restrict expression because of its message, its ideas, its subject matter, or its content." *Ashcroft v. American Civil Liberties Union*, 535 U.S. 564 (2002). There are of course exceptions. "'From 1791 to the present,' . . . the First Amendment has 'permitted restrictions upon the content of speech in a few limited areas,' and has never 'include[d] a freedom to disregard these traditional limitations.'" *United States v. Stevens*, [130 S.Ct. 1577] (2010). These limited areas—such as obscenity, *Roth v. United States*, 354 U.S. 476 483 (1957), incitement, *Brandenburg v. Ohio*, 395 U.S. 444 (1969), and fighting words, *Chaplinsky v. New Hampshire*, 315 U.S. 568 (1942)—represent "well-defined and narrowly limited classes of speech, the prevention and punishment of which have never been thought to raise any Constitutional problem."

Last Term, in *Stevens*, we held that new categories of unprotected speech may not be added to the list by a legislature that concludes certain speech is too harmful to be tolerated. *Stevens* concerned a federal statute purporting to criminalize the creation, sale, or possession of certain depictions of animal cruelty. . . .

That holding controls this case. As in *Stevens*, California has tried to make violent-speech regulation look like obscenity regulation by appending a saving clause required for the latter. That does not suffice. Our cases have been clear that the obscenity exception to the First Amendment does not cover whatever a legislature finds shocking, but only depictions of "sexual conduct," *Miller* [*v. California*, 413 U.S. 15 (1973)]. . . .

California's argument would fare better if there were a longstanding tradition in this country of specially restricting children's access to depictions of violence, but there is none. Certainly the books we give children to read—or read to them when they are younger—contain no shortage of gore. *Grimm's Fairy Tales*, for example, are grim indeed. As her just deserts for trying to poison Snow White, the wicked queen is made to dance in red hot slippers "till she fell dead on the floor, a sad example of envy and jealousy." Cinderella's evil step-sisters have their eyes pecked out by doves. And Hansel and Gretel (children!) kill their captor by baking her in an oven.

High-school reading lists are full of similar fare. Homer's Odysseus blinds Polyphemus the Cyclops by grinding out his eye with a heated stake. . . . And Golding's *Lord of the Flies* recounts how a schoolboy called Piggy is savagely murdered by other children while marooned on an island.

This is not to say that minors' consumption of violent entertainment has never encountered resistance. In the 1800's, dime novels depicting crime and "penny dreadfuls" (named for their price and content) were blamed in some quarters for juvenile delinquency. When motion pictures came along, they became the villains instead. For a time, our Court did permit broad censor-ship of movies because of their capacity to be "used for evil," but we eventually reversed course. *Joseph Burstyn, Inc.* Radio dramas were next, and then came comic books. Many in the late 1940's and early 1950's blamed comic books for fostering a "preoccupation with violence and horror" among the young, leading to a rising juvenile crime rate.

California claims that video games present special problems because they are "interactive," in that the player participates in the violent action on screen and determines its outcome. The latter feature is nothing new: Since at least the publication of *The Adventures of You: Sugarcane Island* in 1969, young read-ers of choose-your-own-adventure stories have been able to make decisions that determine the plot by following instructions about which page to turn to. . . .

Because the Act imposes a restriction on the content of protected speech, it is invalid unless California can demonstrate that it passes strict scrutiny—that is, unless it is justified by a compelling government interest and is narrowly drawn to serve that interest. . . .

California cannot meet that standard.

The State's evidence is not compelling. California relies primarily on the research of Dr. Craig Anderson and a few other research psychologists whose studies purport to show a connection between exposure to violent video games and harmful effects on children. These studies have been rejected by every court to consider them, and with good reason: They do not prove that violent video games cause minors to act aggressively (which would at least be a begin-ning). Instead, "[n]early all of the research is based on correlation, not evidence of causation, and most of the studies suffer from significant, admitted flaws in methodology." They show at best some correlation between exposure to vio-lent entertainment and minuscule real-world effects, such as children's feeling more aggressive or making louder noises in the few minutes after playing a violent game than after playing a nonviolent game. . . .

California's legislation straddles the fence between (1) addressing a seri-ous social problem and (2) helping concerned parents control their children. Both ends are legitimate, but when they affect First Amendment rights they must be pursued by means that are neither seriously underinclusive nor seri-ously overinclusive. See *Church of Lukumi Babalu Aye, Inc. v. Hialeah*, 508 U.S. 520 (1993). As a means of protecting children from portrayals of violence, the legislation is seriously underinclusive, not only because it excludes portrayals other than video games, but also because it permits a parental or avuncular veto. And as a means of assisting concerned parents it is seriously overinclusive because it abridges the First Amendment rights of young people whose parents (and aunts and uncles) think violent video games are a harmless pastime. . . .

☐ *Justice ALITO, with whom THE CHIEF JUSTICE joins, concurring in the judgment.*

In considering the application of unchanging constitutional principles to new and rapidly evolving technology, this Court should proceed with caution. We should make every effort to understand the new technology. We should take into account the possibility that developing technology may have important societal implications that will become apparent only with time. We should not jump to the conclusion that new technology is fundamentally the same as some older thing with which we are familiar. And we should not hastily dismiss the judgment of legislators, who may be in a better position than we are to assess the implications of new technology. The opinion of the Court exhibits none of this caution. . . .

There are reasons to suspect that the experience of playing violent video games just might be very different from reading a book, listening to the radio, or watching a movie or a television show. . . .

Here, the California law does not define "violent video games" with the "narrow specificity" that the Constitution demands. . . . Although our society does not generally regard all depictions of violence as suitable for children or adolescents, the prevalence of violent depictions in children's literature and entertainment creates numerous opportunities for reasonable people to disagree about which depictions may excite "deviant" or "morbid" impulses. . . .

For these reasons, I conclude that the California violent video game law fails to provide the fair notice that the Constitution requires. And I would go no further. I would not express any view on whether a properly drawn statute would or would not survive First Amendment scrutiny. We should address that question only if and when it is necessary to do so. . . .

Today's most advanced video games create realistic alternative worlds in which millions of players immerse themselves for hours on end. These games feature visual imagery and sounds that are strikingly realistic, and in the near future video-game graphics may be virtually indistinguishable from actual video footage. Many of the games already on the market can produce high definition images, and it is predicted that it will not be long before video-game images will be seen in three dimensions. It is also forecast that video games will soon provide sensory feedback. By wearing a special vest or other device, a player will be able to experience physical sensations supposedly felt by a character on the screen. Some *amici* who support respondents foresee the day when "'virtual-reality shoot-'em-ups'" will allow children to "'actually feel the splatting blood from the blown-off head'" of a victim. . . .

For all these reasons, I would hold only that the particular law at issue here fails to provide the clear notice that the Constitution requires. . . . If differently framed statutes are enacted by the States or by the Federal Government, we can consider the constitutionality of those laws when cases challenging them are presented to us.

☐ *Justice THOMAS, dissenting.*

The Court's decision today does not comport with the original public understanding of the First Amendment. The majority strikes down, as facially unconstitutional, a state law that prohibits the direct sale or rental of certain video games to minors because the law "abridg[es] the freedom of speech." But I do not think the First Amendment stretches that far. The practices and beliefs of the founding generation establish that "the freedom of speech," as originally understood, does not include a right to speak to minors (or a right of minors to access speech) without going through the minors' parents or guardians. I would hold that the law at issue is not facially unconstitutional under the First Amendment, and reverse and remand for further proceedings. . . .

As originally understood, the First Amendment's protection against laws "abridging the freedom of speech" did not extend to all speech. "There are certain well-defined and narrowly limited classes of speech, the prevention and punishment of which have never been thought to raise any Constitutional problem." *Chaplinsky v. New Hampshire*, 315 U.S. 568 (1942). Laws regulating such speech do not "abridg[e] the freedom of speech" because such speech is understood to fall outside "the freedom of speech."

In my view, the "practices and beliefs held by the Founders" reveal another category of excluded speech: speech to minor children bypassing their parents. The historical evidence shows that the founding generation believed parents had absolute authority over their minor children and expected parents to use that authority to direct the proper development of their children. It would be absurd to suggest that such a society understood "the freedom of speech" to include a right to speak to minors (or a corresponding right of minors to access speech) without going through the minors' parents. The founding generation would not have considered it an abridgment of "the freedom of speech" to support parental authority by restricting speech that bypasses minors' parents. . . .

In the Puritan tradition common in the New England Colonies, fathers ruled families with absolute authority. The Puritans rejected many customs, such as godparenthood, that they considered inconsistent with the patriarchal structure. Part of the father's absolute power was the right and duty "to fill his children's minds with knowledge and . . . make them apply their knowledge in right action." . . .

Based on these views of childhood, the founding generation understood parents to have a right and duty to govern their children's growth. Parents were expected to direct the development and education of their children and ensure that bad habits did not take root. . . .

The law at the time reflected the founding generation's understanding of parent-child relations. According to Sir William Blackstone, parents were responsible for maintaining, protecting, and educati[ng] their children, and therefore had "power" over their children. *Commentaries on the Laws of England* (1765). . . .

"The freedom of speech," as originally understood, does not include a right to speak to minors without going through the minors' parents or guardians. Therefore, I cannot agree that the statute at issue is facially unconstitutional under the First Amendment.

I respectfully dissent.

□ *Justice BREYER, dissenting.*

The majority's claim that the California statute, if upheld, would create a "new categor[y] of unprotected speech" is overstated. No one here argues that depictions of violence, even extreme violence, *automatically* fall outside the First Amendment's protective scope as, for example, do obscenity and depictions of child pornography. We properly speak of *categories* of expression that lack protection when, like "child pornography," the category is broad, when it applies automatically, and when the State can prohibit everyone, including adults, from obtaining access to the material within it. But where, as here, careful analysis must precede a narrower judicial conclusion (say, denying protection to a shout of "fire" in a crowded theater, or to an effort to teach a terrorist group how to peacefully petition the United Nations), we do not normally describe the result as creating a "new category of unprotected speech." . . .

The interest that California advances in support of the statute is compelling. . . . As to the need to help parents guide their children, the Court noted in 1968 that "parental control or guidance cannot always be provided." Today, 5.3 million grade-school-age children of working parents are routinely home alone. Thus, it has, if anything, become more important to supplement parents' authority to guide their children's development.

As to the State's independent interest, we have pointed out that juveniles are more likely to show a "lack of maturity" and are "more vulnerable or susceptible to negative influences and outside pressures," and that their "character . . . is not as well formed as that of an adult." *Roper v. Simmons*, 543 U.S. 551 (2005). And we have therefore recognized "a compelling interest in protecting the physical and psychological well-being of minors."

At the same time, there is considerable evidence that California's statute significantly furthers this compelling interest. . . . There are many scientific studies that support California's views. Social scientists, for example, have found *causal* evidence that playing these games results in harm. Longitudinal studies, which measure changes over time, have found that increased exposure to violent video games causes an increase in aggression over the same period.

Experimental studies in laboratories have found that subjects randomly assigned to play a violent video game subsequently displayed more characteristics of aggression than those who played nonviolent games.

Surveys of 8th and 9th grade students have found a correlation between playing violent video games and aggression.

And "meta-analysis," *i.e.*, studies of all the studies, have concluded that exposure to violent video games "was positively associated with aggressive behavior, aggressive cognition, and aggressive affect," and that "playing violent video games is a *causal* risk factor for long-term harmful outcomes."

The upshot is that California's statute, as applied to its heartland of applications (*i.e.*, buyers under 17; extremely violent, realistic video games), imposes a restriction on speech that is modest at most. That restriction is justified by a compelling interest (supplementing parents' efforts to prevent their children from purchasing potentially harmful violent, interactive material). And there is no equally effective, less restrictive alternative. California's statute is consequently constitutional on its face—though litigants remain free to challenge the statute as applied in particular instances, including any effort by the State to apply it to minors aged 17. . . .

For these reasons, I respectfully dissent.

D | *Commercial Speech*

■ THE DEVELOPMENT OF LAW

Other Important Rulings on Commercial Speech and the First Amendment

CASE	VOTE	RULING
Sorrell v. IMS Health Inc., 131 S.Ct. 2653 (2011)	6:3	Writing for the Court, Justice Kennedy invalidated Vermont's Prescription Confidentiality Law

of 2007, restricting the disclosure and sale of pharmacy records that reveal the prescribing practices of individual doctors. The law was challenged by some pharmaceutical manufacturers and "data mining" firms which collect such data and analyze it to produce reports on prescribers' behavior. Data miners lease these reports to pharmaceutical manufacturers, whose sales representatives use the reports to refine their marketing tactics and to increase sales. The majority held that, "[s]peech in aid of pharmaceutical marketing . . . is a form of expression protected by the Free Speech Clause of the First Amendment," because it is a content-based restriction aimed at particular speakers and cannot satisfy "heightened judicial scrutiny." In Justice Kennedy's words: "The Constitution 'does not enact Mr. Herbert Spencer's *Social Statics.' Lochner v. New York* (1905) (Holmes, J., dissenting). It does enact the First Amendment." Justices Breyer, Ginsburg, and Kagan dissented.

F | *Regulating the Broadcast and Cable Media, and the Internet*

The Court revisited the Federal Communication Commission's (FCC) enforcement of its "indecency standard" in *FCC v. Fox Television Stations, Inc.* In 2004, the FCC modified its indecency policy to include the broadcasting of "fleeting" expletives, punishable by fines. Fox and all other major broadcasting networks challenged the constitutionality of new policy. The Court of Appeals for the Second Circuit held that the policy change was arbitrary and capricious under the Administrative Procedures Act (APA) because the FCC did not provide adequate reasons for its change in policy. On appeal that decision was reversed by the Supreme Court, in *FCC v. Fox Television Stations*, 129 S.Ct. 1800 (2009) (*Fox Television I*), and remanded to the appellate court for consideration of the constitutionality of the policy change. On remand, the Second Circuit held that the FCC's policy was unconstitutional and impermissibly vague in failing to provide fair notice, because the networks were forced to choose between airing a program and risking a fine based on the policy, or not airing the program at all. That choice, the appellate court concluded, had a "chilling effect" on First Amendment freedoms. When the Roberts Court revisited the controversy in *FCC v. Fox Television Stations*, 132 S.Ct. 2307 (2012) (*Fox Television II*), however, it avoided the First Amendment controversy and instead held that the FCC failed to give Fox and ABC fair notice about fleeting expletives and momentary nudity would be indecent. In other words, the FCC's standards were vague and the Court for a second time would not reconsider its original ruling on the FCC's "indecency standard" in *FCC v. Pacifica Foundation*, 438 U.S. 726 (1978) (excerpted in Vol. 2, Ch. 5).

H | *Symbolic Speech and Speech-Plus-Conduct*

(2) *Speech-Plus-Conduct*

In a widely watched and emotional case, *Snyder v. Phelps* (2011) (excerpted below), the Court upheld First Amendment protection for picketers at military funerals in protest of tolerance for homosexuals, particularly in the military. Although reaffirming broad First Amendment protection for freedom of expression, the Court's opinion was notably narrowly tailored to the facts in the case.

Snyder v. Phelps
131 S.Ct. 1207 (2011)

Fred Phelps founded the Westboro Baptist Church, a small family-run church, in Topeka, Kansas, in 1955. The church preaches that God hates and punishes the United States for its tolerance of homosexuality, particularly in the military. During the last 20 years the church has publicized its message by picketing nearly 600 military funerals. One of those was for Marine Lance Corporal Matthew Snyder, who was killed in Iraq. Phelps read about Snyder's funeral and decided to travel to Maryland with six other Westboro Baptist parishioners to picket. The church notified authorities in advance of its intent and complied with police instructions in picketing, which took place within a 10- by 25-foot plot of public land adjacent to a public street, behind a temporary fence, approximately 1,000 feet from where the funeral was held. Several buildings also separated the picket site from the funeral and none of the picketers went into the cemetery.

Albert Snyder, the father of Matthew Snyder, objected and sued Phelps and the church for the tort of infliction of emotional distress, though he later testified that he could only see the tops of the picket signs as he drove to the funeral; he did not see what was written on the signs until later that night when watching a news broadcast covering the funeral. Phelps in turn countered that the demonstration was protected by the First Amendment. A jury found for Snyder and awarded ten million dollars in damages, which a federal district court reduced to two million. On appeal, the Court of Appeals for the Fourth Circuit reversed and held that the picketing was First Amendment-protected speech.

On appeal, the Supreme Court by an eight-to-one vote affirmed the appellate court. Chief Justice Roberts delivered the opinion for the Court, while Justice Breyer filed a concurrence, and Justice Alito filed a dissenting opinion.

☐ *CHIEF JUSTICE ROBERTS delivered the opinion of the Court.*

Whether the First Amendment prohibits holding Westboro liable for its speech in this case turns largely on whether that speech is of public or private concern, as determined by all the circumstances of the case. "[S]peech on 'matters of public concern' . . . is 'at the heart of the First Amendment's protection.'" *Dun & Bradstreet, Inc. v. Greenmoss Builders, Inc.*, 472 U.S. 749 (1985). . . .

Our opinion in *Dun & Bradstreet*, on the other hand, provides an example of speech of only private concern. In that case we held, as a general matter, that information about a particular individual's credit report "concerns no public issue." The content of the report, we explained, "was speech solely in the individual interest of the speaker and its specific business audience." That was confirmed by the fact that the particular report was sent to only five subscribers to the reporting service, who were bound not to disseminate it further.

Deciding whether speech is of public or private concern requires us to examine the "'content, form, and context'" of that speech, "'as revealed by the whole record.'" *Dun & Bradstreet.* The "content" of Westboro's signs plainly relates to broad issues of interest to society at large, rather than matters of "purely private concern." The placards read "God Hates the USA/Thank God for 9/11," "America is Doomed," "Don't Pray for the USA," "Thank God for IEDs," "Fag Troops," "Semper Fi Fags," "God Hates Fags," "Maryland Taliban," "Fags Doom Nations," "Not Blessed Just Cursed," "Thank God for Dead Soldiers," "Pope in Hell," "Priests Rape Boys," "You're Going to Hell," and "God Hates You." While these messages may fall short of refined social or political commentary, the issues they highlight—the political and moral conduct of the United States and its citizens, the fate of our Nation, homosexuality in the military, and scandals involving the Catholic clergy—are matters of public import. . . .

Apart from the content of Westboro's signs, Snyder contends that the "context" of the speech—its connection with his son's funeral—makes the speech a matter of private rather than public concern. The fact that Westboro spoke in connection with a funeral, however, cannot by itself transform the nature of Westboro's speech. Westboro's signs, displayed on public land next to a public street, reflect the fact that the church finds much to condemn in modern society. Its speech is "fairly characterized as constituting speech on a matter of public concern," and the funeral setting does not alter that conclusion. . . .

Simply put, the church members had the right to be where they were. Westboro alerted local authorities to its funeral protest and fully complied with police guidance on where the picketing could be staged. The picketing was conducted under police supervision some 1,000 feet from the church, out of the sight of those at the church. The protest was not unruly; there was no shouting, profanity, or violence.

For all these reasons, the jury verdict imposing tort liability on Westboro for intentional infliction of emotional distress must be set aside. . . .

☐ *Justice ALITO, dissenting.*

Respondents and other members of their church have strong opinions on certain moral, religious, and political issues. . . . And they may express their views in terms that are "uninhibited," "vehement," and "caustic." *New York Times Co. v. Sullivan*, 376 U.S. 254 (1964).

It does not follow, however, that they may intentionally inflict severe emotional injury on private persons at a time of intense emotional sensitivity by launching vicious verbal attacks that make no contribution to public debate. To protect against such injury, "most if not all jurisdictions" permit recovery in tort for the intentional infliction of emotional distress (or IIED). *Hustler Magazine, Inc. v. Falwell*, 485 U.S. 46 (1988). . . .

In light of [the facts], it is abundantly clear that respondents, going far beyond commentary on matters of public concern, specifically attacked Matthew Snyder because (1) he was a Catholic and (2) he was a member of the United States military. Both Matthew and petitioner were private figures, and this attack was not speech on a matter of public concern. While commentary on the Catholic Church or the United States military constitutes speech on matters of public concern, speech regarding Matthew Snyder's purely private conduct does not. . . .

Respondents' outrageous conduct caused petitioner great injury, and the Court now compounds that injury by depriving petitioner of a judgment that acknowledges the wrong he suffered.

In order to have a society in which public issues can be openly and vigorously debated, it is not necessary to allow the brutalization of innocent victims like petitioner. I therefore respectfully dissent.

6

Freedom from and of Religion

A | The (Dis)establishment of Religion

In a major ruling on freedom of religion in *Hosanna-Tabor Evangelical Lutheran Church and School v. Equal Employment Opportunity Commission*, 132 S.Ct. 694 (2012), the Court unanimously held that the Americans With Disabilities Act does not apply to employees who perform religious duties for religious organizations, and that the latter have a broad constitutional right to select and fire their own leaders. Writing for the Court, Chief Justice Roberts recognized a broad "ministerial exception" to anti-discrimination laws that is rooted in the combined purposes of the First Amendment (Dis)establishment Clause and the Free Exercise Clause to separate government from the religion. As a result, employees of religious organizations who perform "ministerial" functions as defined by a religious school or organization may not sue the religious employer for allegedly violating the Americans With Disabilities Act in its employment decisions. Cheryl Perich was a designated commissioned minister who at Hosanna-Tabor Evangelical Lutheran Church and School taught secular subjects, along with religion classes and led her students in daily prayers. Perich developed narcolepsy and went on disability leave. But when she wanted to return, the school informed her that she had been replaced. When she threatened to sue the school for violating the Americans With Disabilities Act, the school maintained that as a teacher and a minister Perich was subject to the "ministerial exception" exempting religious organizations and their employment decisions from compliance with anti-discrimination laws, because of the First Amendment guarantees for religious freedom. In separate concurring opinions

Justices Thomas and Alito would have, respectively, adopted a broader and somewhat narrower "ministerial exception."

In its 2013–2014 term, the Roberts Court will reconsider whether legislative prayers violate the First Amendment in *Town of Greece v. Galloway* (Docket No. 12–696). The Town of Greece, New York, opened all board meetings with a legislative prayer and would invite a member of the community, based on a community guide published in the local paper, to conduct a prayer prior to each meeting. A majority of the prayer givers were Christians, and the town was challenged for violating the First Amendment (Dis)establishment Clause. The lower court held that the legislative prayer was a violation of the First Amendment because when viewed by a reasonable observer the consistent prayer by one faith was an endorsement of religion by the state. The Town of Greece appealed and the Supreme Court granted *certiorari* in order to determine whether the legislative prayer runs afoul of the First Amendment.

7

THE FOURTH AMENDMENT GUARANTEE AGAINST UNREASONABLE SEARCHES AND SEIZURES

In a bitter five-to-four decision, the Court held that police may take DNA swabs from suspects arrested (but not yet tried and convicted) for "serious" violent crimes. Writing for the Court in *Maryland v. King*, 133 S.Ct. 1958 (2013), Justice Kennedy likened the DNA samples to fingerprinting during a suspect's booking as "a safe and secure way to process and identify the persons and possessions they must take into custody." Justice Kennedy rejected privacy claims, observing that "once an individual has been arrested on probable cause for a dangerous offense that may require detention before trial, his or her expectations of privacy and freedom from police scrutiny are reduced." By contrast, dissenting Justice Scalia, joined by Justices Ginsburg, Sotomayor, and Kagan, countered that the DNA swabs amounted to a general search warrant in order to possibly solve "cold cases" and thus lacked reasonable individualized suspicion. Alonzo Jay King Jr. was arrested for assault and police took a DNA sample that ultimately linked him to a six-year-old unresolved rape case, for which he was subsequently tried, convicted, and sentenced to life imprisonment.

A | *Requirements for a Warrant and Reasonable Searches and Seizures*

The Roberts Court's first encounter with the Fourth Amendment's application in the digital age of the twenty-first century left more questions unanswered than addressed and, thus, invited decades of litigation. Moreover, although unanimous in the ruling the Court actually split four to four to one and decided the narrowest—minimalist—question. Justice Scalia's opinion for the Court commanded only the support of a plurality—Chief Justice Roberts and Justices Kennedy and Thomas— in holding that the planting of a global positioning system (GPS) tracking device on a car for almost a month constituted a "search" for Fourth Amendment purposes. The opinion turned on the fact that a trespass on private property was involved and only secondarily did "reasonable expectations of privacy" come into consideration. By contrast, Justice Alito's concurrence, joined by Justices Ginsburg, Breyer, and Kagan, did not concede that a "search" had occurred and quarreled with that focus of analysis, emphasizing instead that the issue should be analyzed in terms of "reasonable expectations of privacy" under the amendment. Neither Justice Scalia's opinion for the Court nor Justice Alito's concurrence, however, reached the issue of whether a warrant or probable cause, or a "reasonable suspicion" of criminality, was required. Both also held out the possibility that the warrantless installation of GPS devices might be permissible depending on the length of the period of tracking and/or the investigatory purpose (e.g., monitoring drug trafficking versus combating potential terrorist attacks). In a separate concurring opinion, Justice Sotomayor indicated the need to reassess privacy in light of twenty-first century developments but joined in the ruling because it was all that was needed to dispose of the case, *United States v. Jones* (2012) (excerpted below).

In its 2012–2013 term, a bare majority of the Court underscored the Fourth Amendment's protection for homes in *Florida v. Jardines* (2013) (excerpted below), in contrast to *Florida v. Harris*, 133 S.Ct. 1409 (2013) (discussed in Section C of this chapter). Note that Justice Scalia's opinion for the Court relies on traditional trespass theory on a "constitutionally protected area," whereas Justice Kagan's concurrence would reach the same result based on an analysis of "reasonable expectations of privacy," while the dissenters reject both approaches.

United States v. Jones
132 S.Ct. 945 (2012)

Antoine Jones, the owner of a nightclub in the District of Columbia, was the target of a law enforcement investigation of drug trafficking. Officers used various investigative techniques, including visual surveillance and the installation of a camera focused on the front door of the nightclub, a pen register (to record the numbers of telephone calls), and a wiretap covering Jones's cellular phone. Based on those sources, the government sought a warrant authorizing the use of a Global Positioning System (GPS) electronic tracking device for the Jeep Grand Cherokee registered to Jones's wife. A warrant was issued for the installation of the GPS device in the District of Columbia within 10 days. However, not until the 11th day, and not in the District of Columbia but in Maryland, did agents install the device on the undercarriage of the Jeep while parked in a public parking lot. Over the next 28 days, agents tracked the Jeep's movements and once replaced the device's battery when the vehicle was in a public lot in Maryland. The device tracked the Jeep's location within 50 to 100 feet and transmitted that location by cellular phone to a government computer. The government ultimately obtained a multiple-count indictment charging Jones with conspiracy to distribute cocaine. Before trial, Jones filed a motion to suppress evidence obtained through the GPS device. The district court granted the motion in part, suppressing the data obtained while the vehicle was parked in the garage adjoining Jones's residence but holding the remaining data admissible, because "'[a] person traveling in an automobile on public thoroughfares has no reasonable expectation of privacy in his movements from one place to another.'" Jones's trial ended with a hung jury, but a second trial found him guilty and he was sentenced to life imprisonment. On appeal, however, the United States Court of Appeals for the District of Columbia Circuit reversed on the ground that the conviction based on the warrantless use of the GPS device violated the Fourth Amendment. The government appealed and the Supreme Court granted *certiorari*.

The appellate court's decision was affirmed. Justice Scalia delivered the opinion for the Court. Justices Alito and Sotomayor each filed concurring opinions; Justices Ginsburg, Breyer, and Kagan joined Justice Alito's concurrence.

☐ *Justice SCALIA delivered the opinion of the Court.*

The Fourth Amendment provides in relevant part that "[t]he right of the people to be secure in their persons, houses, papers, and effects, against unreasonable searches and seizures, shall not be violated." It is beyond dispute that a vehicle is an "effect" as that term is used in the Amendment. We hold that the Government's installation of a GPS device on a target's vehicle, and its use of that device to monitor the vehicle's movements, constitutes a "search."

It is important to be clear about what occurred in this case: The Government physically occupied private property for the purpose of obtaining information. We have no doubt that such a physical intrusion would have been considered a "search" within the meaning of the Fourth Amendment when it was adopted. *Entick v. Carrington*, 95 Eng. Rep. 807 (C. P. 1765), is a "case we have described as a 'monument of English freedom' 'undoubtedly familiar' to 'every American statesman' at the time the Constitution was adopted, and considered to be 'the true and ultimate expression of constitutional law'" with regard to search and seizure. In that case, Lord Camden expressed in plain terms the significance of property rights in search-and-seizure analysis: "[O]ur law holds the property of every man so sacred, that no man can set his foot upon his neighbour's close without his leave; if he does he is a trespasser, though he does no damage at all; if he will tread upon his neighbour's ground, he must justify it by law."

The text of the Fourth Amendment reflects its close connection to property, since otherwise it would have referred simply to "the right of the people to be secure against unreasonable searches and seizures"; the phrase "in their persons, houses, papers, and effects" would have been superfluous.

Consistent with this understanding, our Fourth Amendment jurisprudence was tied to common-law trespass, at least until the latter half of the 20th century. Thus, in *Olmstead v. United States*, 277 U.S. 438 (1928), we held that wiretaps attached to telephone wires on the public streets did not constitute a Fourth Amendment search because "[t]here was no entry of the houses or offices of the defendants."

Our later cases, of course, have deviated from that exclusively property-based approach. In *Katz v. United States*, 389 U.S. 347 (1967), we said that "the Fourth Amendment protects people, not places," and found a violation in attachment of an eavesdropping device to a public telephone booth. Our later cases have applied the analysis of Justice HARLAN's concurrence in that case, which said that a violation occurs when government officers violate a person's "reasonable expectation of privacy." The Government contends that the HARLAN standard shows that no search occurred here, since Jones had no "reasonable expectation of privacy" in the area of the Jeep accessed by Government agents (its underbody) and in the locations of the Jeep on the public roads, which were visible to all. But we need not address the Government's contentions, because Jones's Fourth Amendment rights do not rise or fall with the *Katz* formulation. At bottom, we must "assur[e] preservation of that degree of privacy against government that existed when the Fourth Amendment was adopted." *Kyllo* [*v. United States*, 533 U.S. 27 (2001)]. As explained, for most of our history the Fourth Amendment was understood to embody a particular concern for government trespass upon the areas ("persons, houses, papers, and effects") it enumerates.

Katz did not repudiate that understanding. . . . *Katz* did not narrow the Fourth Amendment's scope. The Government contends that several of our post-*Katz* cases foreclose the conclusion that what occurred here constituted a search. It relies principally on two cases in which we rejected Fourth Amendment challenges to "beepers," electronic tracking devices that represent another form of electronic monitoring. The first case, [*United States v.*] *Knotts*, [460 U.S. 276 (1983)], upheld against Fourth Amendment challenge the use of a "beeper" that had been placed in a container of chloroform, allowing law enforcement to monitor the location of the container. We said that there had been no infringement of Knotts' reasonable expectation of privacy since the information obtained—the location of the automobile carrying the container on public roads, and the location of the off-loaded container in open fields near Knotts' cabin—had been voluntarily conveyed to the public. But as we have discussed, the *Katz* reasonable-expectation-of-privacy test has been added to, not substituted for, the common-law trespassory test. . . . The second "beeper" case, *United States v. Karo*, 468 U.S. 705 (1984), does not suggest a different conclusion. . . .

Finally, the Government's position gains little support from our conclusion in *Oliver v. United States*, 466 U.S. 170 (1984), that officers' information-gathering intrusion on an "open field" did not constitute a Fourth Amendment search even though it was a trespass at common law. Quite simply, an open field, unlike the curtilage of a home, is not one of those protected areas enumerated in the Fourth Amendment. The Government's physical intrusion on such an area—unlike its intrusion on the "effect" at issue here—is of no Fourth Amendment significance.

The concurrence begins by accusing us of applying "18th-century tort law." That is a distortion. What we apply is an 18th-century guarantee against unreasonable searches, which we believe must provide at a minimum the degree of protection it afforded when it was adopted. The concurrence does not share that belief. It would apply exclusively *Katz*'s reasonable-expectation-of-privacy test, even when that eliminates rights that previously existed.

The concurrence faults our approach for "present[ing] particularly vexing problems" in cases that do not involve physical contact, such as those that involve the transmission of electronic signals. We entirely fail to understand that point. For unlike the concurrence, which would make *Katz* the exclusive test, we do not make trespass the exclusive test. Situations involving merely the transmission of electronic signals without trespass would remain subject to *Katz* analysis.

In fact, it is the concurrence's insistence on the exclusivity of the *Katz* test that needlessly leads us into "particularly vexing problems" in the present case. This Court has to date not deviated from the understanding that mere visual observation does not constitute a search. . . . Thus, even assuming that the concurrence is correct to say that "[t]raditional surveillance" of Jones for a 4-week period "would have required a large team of agents, multiple vehicles, and perhaps aerial assistance," our cases suggest that such visual observation is constitutionally permissible. It may be that achieving the same result through electronic means, without an accompanying trespass, is an unconstitutional invasion of privacy, but the present case does not require us to answer that question. And answering it affirmatively leads us needlessly into additional thorny problems. The concurrence posits that "relatively short-term monitoring of a person's movements on public streets" is okay, but that "the use of longer term GPS monitoring in investigations of most offenses" is no good. That introduces yet another novelty into our jurisprudence.

There is no precedent for the proposition that whether a search has occurred depends on the nature of the crime being investigated. And even accepting that novelty, it remains unexplained why a 4-week investigation is "surely" too long and why a drug-trafficking conspiracy involving substantial amounts of cash and narcotics is not an "extra-ordinary offens[e]" which may permit longer observation. What of a 2-day monitoring of a suspected purveyor of stolen electronics? Or of a 6-month monitoring of a suspected terrorist? We may have to grapple with these "vexing problems" in some future case where a classic trespassory search is not involved and resort must be had to *Katz* analysis; but there is no reason for rushing forward to resolve them here. . . .

☐ *Justice ALITO, with whom Justice GINSBURG, Justice BREYER, and Justice KAGAN join, concurring in the judgment.*

This case requires us to apply the Fourth Amendment's prohibition of unreasonable searches and seizures to a 21st-century surveillance technique, the use of a Global Positioning System (GPS) device to monitor a vehicle's movements for an extended period of time. Ironically, the Court has chosen to decide this case based on 18th-century tort law. By attaching a small GPS device to the underside of the vehicle that respondent drove, the law enforcement officers in this case engaged in conduct that might have provided grounds in 1791 for a suit for trespass to chattels. And for this reason, the Court concludes, the installation and use of the GPS device constituted a search.

This holding, in my judgment, is unwise. It strains the language of the Fourth Amendment; it has little if any support in current Fourth Amendment case law; and it is highly artificial. I would analyze the question presented in this case by asking whether respondent's reasonable expectations of privacy were violated by the long-term monitoring of the movements of the vehicle he drove.

The Fourth Amendment prohibits "unreasonable searches and seizures," and the Court makes very little effort to explain how the attachment or use of the GPS device fits within these terms. The Court does not contend that there was a seizure. . . .

The Court does claim that the installation and use of the GPS constituted a search, but this conclusion is dependent on the questionable proposition that these two procedures cannot be separated for purposes of Fourth Amendment analysis. If these two procedures are analyzed separately, it is not at all clear from the Court's opinion why either should be regarded as a search.

It is clear that the attachment of the GPS device was not itself a search; if the device had not functioned or if the officers had not used it, no information would have been obtained. And the Court does not contend that the use of the device constituted a search either. On the contrary, the Court accepts the holding in *United States v. Knotts*, 460 U.S. 276 (1983), that the use of a surreptitiously planted electronic device to monitor a vehicle's movements on public roads did not amount to a search.

The Court argues—and I agree—that "we must 'assur[e] preservation of that degree of privacy against government that existed when the Fourth Amendment was adopted.'" But it is almost impossible to think of late-18th-century situations that are analogous to what took place in this case. . . . The Court's theory seems to be that the concept of a search, as originally understood, comprehended any technical trespass that led to the gathering of evidence, but we know that this is incorrect. At common law, any unauthorized intrusion on private property was actionable, but a trespass on open fields, as opposed to the "curtilage" of a home, does not fall within the scope of the Fourth Amendment because private property outside the curtilage is not part of a "hous[e]" within the meaning of the Fourth Amendment.

The Court's reasoning in this case is very similar to that in the Court's early decisions involving wiretapping and electronic eavesdropping, namely, that a technical trespass followed by the gathering of evidence constitutes a search. In the early electronic surveillance cases, the Court concluded that a Fourth Amendment search occurred when private conversations were monitored as a result of an "unauthorized physical penetration into the premises occupied" by the defendant. *Silverman v. United States*, 365 U.S. 505 (1961). In *Silverman*, police officers listened to conversations in an attached home by inserting a "spike mike" through the wall that this house shared with the vacant house next door. This procedure was held to be a search because the mike made contact with a heating duct on the other side of the wall and thus "usurp[ed] . . . an integral part of the premises."

By contrast, in cases in which there was no trespass, it was held that there was no search. Thus, in *Olmstead v. United States* (1928), the Court found that the Fourth Amendment did not apply because "[t]he taps from house lines were made in the streets near the houses." Similarly, the Court concluded that no search occurred in *Goldman v. United States*, 316 U.S. 129 (1942), where a "detectaphone" was placed on the outer wall of defendant's office for the purpose of overhearing conversations held within the room.

This trespass-based rule was repeatedly criticized. In *Olmstead*, Justice BRANDEIS wrote that it was "immaterial where the physical connection with the telephone wires was made." Although a private conversation transmitted by wire did not fall within the literal words of the Fourth Amendment, he argued, the Amendment should be understood as prohibiting "every unjustifiable intrusion by the government upon the privacy of the individual."

Katz v. United States finally did away with the old approach, holding that a trespass was not required for a Fourth Amendment violation. *Katz* involved the use of a listening device that was attached to the outside of a public telephone booth and that allowed police officers to eavesdrop on one end of the target's phone conversation. This procedure did not physically intrude on the area occupied by the target, but the *Katz* Court "repudiate[ed]" the old doctrine and held that "[t]he fact that the electronic device employed . . . did not happen to penetrate the wall of the booth can have no constitutional significance." What mattered, the Court now held, was whether the conduct at issue "violated the privacy upon which [the defendant] justifiably relied while using the telephone booth." Under this approach, as the Court later put it when addressing the relevance of a technical trespass, "an actual trespass is neither necessary nor sufficient to establish a constitutional violation." *United States v. Karo*, 468 U.S. 705 (1984). . . .

In sum, the majority is hard pressed to find support in post-*Katz* cases for its trespass-based theory. Disharmony with a substantial body of existing case law is only one of the problems with the Court's approach in this case. I will briefly note four others.

First, the Court's reasoning largely disregards what is really important (the use of a GPS for the purpose of long-term tracking) and instead attaches great significance to something that most would view as relatively minor (attaching to the bottom of a car a small, light object that does not interfere in any way with the car's operation). Attaching such an object is generally regarded as so trivial that it does not provide a basis for recovery under modern tort law. But under the Court's reasoning, this conduct may violate the Fourth Amendment. By contrast, if long-term monitoring can be accomplished without committing a technical trespass—suppose, for example, that the Federal Government required or persuaded auto manufacturers to include a GPS tracking device in every car—the Court's theory would provide no protection.

Second, the Court's approach leads to incongruous results. If the police attach a GPS device to a car and use the device to follow the car for even a brief time, under the Court's theory, the Fourth Amendment applies. But if the police follow the same car for a much longer period using unmarked cars and aerial assistance, this tracking is not subject to any Fourth Amendment constraints. In the present case, the Fourth Amendment applies, the Court concludes, because the officers installed the GPS device after respondent's wife, to whom the car was registered, turned it over to respondent for his exclusive use. But if the GPS had been attached prior to that time, the Court's theory would lead to a different result. The Court proceeds on the assumption that respondent "had at least the property rights of a bailee," but a bailee may sue for a trespass to chattel only if the injury occurs during the term of the bailment. So if the GPS device had been installed before respondent's wife gave him the keys, respondent would have no claim for trespass—and, presumably, no Fourth Amendment claim either.

Third, under the Court's theory, the coverage of the Fourth Amendment may vary from State to State. If the events at issue here had occurred in a community property State or a State that has adopted the Uniform Marital Property Act, respondent would likely be an owner of the vehicle, and it would not matter whether the GPS was installed before or after his wife turned over the keys. In non-community-property States, on the other hand, the registration of the vehicle in the name of respondent's wife would generally be regarded as presumptive evidence that she was the sole owner.

Fourth, the Court's reliance on the law of trespass will present particularly vexing problems in cases involving surveillance that is carried out by making electronic, as opposed to physical, contact with the item to be tracked. For example, suppose that the officers in the present case had followed respondent by surreptitiously activating a stolen vehicle detection system that came with the car when it was purchased. Would the sending of a radio signal to activate this system constitute a trespass to chattels? Trespass to chattels has traditionally required a physical touching of the property. In recent years, courts have wrestled with the application of this old tort in cases involving unwanted electronic contact with computer systems, and some have held that even the transmission of electrons that occurs when a communication is sent from one computer to another is enough. But may such decisions be followed in applying the Court's trespass theory? Assuming that what matters under the Court's theory is the law of trespass as it existed at the time of the adoption of the Fourth Amendment, do these recent decisions represent a change in the law or simply the application of the old tort to new situations?

The *Katz* expectation-of-privacy test avoids the problems and complications noted above, but it is not without its own difficulties. It involves a degree of circularity, and judges are apt to confuse their own expectations of privacy with those of the hypothetical reasonable person to which the *Katz* test looks. In addition, the *Katz* test rests on the assumption that this hypothetical reasonable person has a well-developed and stable set of privacy expectations. But technology can change those expectations. Dramatic technological change may lead to periods in which popular expectations are in flux and may ultimately produce significant changes in popular attitudes. New technology may provide increased convenience or security at the expense of privacy, and many people may find the tradeoff worthwhile. And even if the public does not welcome the diminution of privacy that new technology entails, they may eventually reconcile themselves to this development as inevitable. . . .

Recent years have seen the emergence of many new devices that permit the monitoring of a person's movements. In some locales, closed-circuit television video monitoring is becoming ubiquitous. On toll roads, automatic toll collection systems create a precise record of the movements of motorists who choose to make use of that convenience. Many motorists purchase cars that are equipped with devices that permit a central station to ascertain the car's location at any time so that roadside assistance may be provided if needed and the car may be found if it is stolen.

In the pre-computer age, the greatest protections of privacy were neither constitutional nor statutory, but practical. Traditional surveillance for any extended period of time was difficult and costly and therefore rarely undertaken. The surveillance at issue in this case—constant monitoring of the location of a vehicle for four weeks—would have required a large team of agents, multiple vehicles, and perhaps aerial assistance. Only an investigation of unusual importance could have justified such an expenditure of law enforcement resources. Devices like the one used in the present case, however, make long-term monitoring relatively easy and cheap. In circumstances involving dramatic technological change, the best solution to privacy concerns may be legislative. A legislative body is well situated to gauge changing public attitudes, to draw detailed lines, and to balance privacy and public safety in a comprehensive way. To date, however, Congress and most States have not enacted statutes regulating the use of GPS tracking technology for law enforcement purposes. The best that we can do in this case is to apply existing Fourth Amendment doctrine and to ask whether the use of GPS tracking in a particular case involved a degree of intrusion that a reasonable person would not have anticipated. Under this approach, relatively short-term monitoring of a person's movements on public streets accords with expectations of privacy that our society has recognized as reasonable. But the use of longer-term GPS monitoring in investigations of most offenses impinges on expectations of privacy. For such offenses, society's expectation has been that law enforcement agents and others would not—and indeed, in the main, simply could not—secretly monitor and catalogue every single movement of an individual's car for a very long period. In this case, for four weeks, law enforcement agents tracked every movement that respondent made in the vehicle he was driving. We need not identify with precision the point at which the tracking of this vehicle became a search, for the line was surely crossed before the 4-week mark. Other cases may present more difficult questions. But where uncertainty exists with respect to whether a certain period of GPS surveillance is long enough to constitute a Fourth Amendment search, the police may always seek a warrant. We also need not consider whether prolonged GPS monitoring in the context of investigations involving extraordinary offenses would similarly intrude on a constitutionally protected sphere of privacy. In such cases, long-term tracking might have been mounted using previously available techniques.

For these reasons, I conclude that the lengthy monitoring that occurred in this case constituted a search under the Fourth Amendment. I therefore agree with the majority that the decision of the Court of Appeals must be affirmed.

☐ *Justice SOTOMAYOR, concurring.*

I join the Court's opinion because I agree that a search within the meaning of the Fourth Amendment occurs, at a minimum, "[w]here, as here, the Government obtains information by physically intruding on a constitutionally protected area." . . .

Of course, the Fourth Amendment is not concerned only with trespassory intrusions on property. Rather, even in the absence of a trespass, "a Fourth Amendment search occurs when the government violates a subjective expectation of privacy that society recognizes as reasonable." In *Katz*, this Court enlarged its then-prevailing focus on property rights by announcing that the reach of the Fourth Amendment does not "turn upon the presence or absence of a physical intrusion." As the majority's opinion makes clear, however, *Katz*'s reasonable-expectation-of-privacy test augmented, but did not displace or diminish, the common-law trespassory test that preceded it. Thus, "when the Government *does* engage in physical intrusion of a constitutionally protected area in order to obtain information, that intrusion may constitute a violation of the Fourth Amendment." *United States v. Knotts*, 460 U.S. 276 (1983) (BRENNAN, J., concurring in judgment). Justice ALITO's approach, which discounts altogether the constitutional relevance of the Government's physical intrusion on Jones' Jeep, erodes that longstanding protection for privacy expectations inherent in items of property that people possess or control. By contrast, the trespassory test applied in the majority's opinion reflects an irreducible constitutional minimum: When the Government physically invades personal property to gather information, a search occurs. The reaffirmation of that principle suffices to decide this case.

Nonetheless, as Justice ALITO notes, physical intrusion is now unnecessary to many forms of surveillance. With increasing regularity, the Government will be capable of duplicating the monitoring undertaken in this case by enlisting factory- or owner-installed vehicle tracking devices or GPS-enabled smartphones. In cases of electronic or other novel modes of surveillance that do not depend upon a physical invasion on property, the majority opinion's trespassory test may provide little guidance. But "[s]ituations involving merely the transmission of electronic signals without trespass would *remain* subject to *Katz* analysis." As Justice ALITO incisively observes, the same technological advances that have made possible nontrespassory surveillance techniques will also affect the *Katz* test by shaping the evolution of societal privacy expectations. Under that rubric, I agree with Justice ALITO that, at the very least, "longer term GPS monitoring in investigations of most offenses impinges on expectations of privacy."

In cases involving even short-term monitoring, some unique attributes of GPS surveillance relevant to the *Katz* analysis will require particular attention. GPS monitoring generates a precise, comprehensive record of a person's public movements that reflects a wealth of detail about her familial, political, professional, religious, and sexual associations. The Government can store such records and efficiently mine them for information years into the future. And because GPS monitoring is cheap in comparison to conventional surveillance techniques and, by design, proceeds surreptitiously, it evades the ordinary checks that constrain abusive law enforcement practices: "limited police resources and community hostility." *Illinois v. Lidster*, 540 U.S. 419 (2004).

Awareness that the Government may be watching chills associational and expressive freedoms. And the Government's unrestrained power to assemble data that reveal private aspects of identity is susceptible to abuse. The net result is that GPS monitoring—by making available at a relatively low cost such a substantial quantum of intimate information about any person whom the Government, in its unfettered discretion, chooses to track—may "alter the relationship between citizen and government in a way that is inimical to democratic society."

I would take these attributes of GPS monitoring into account when considering the existence of a reasonable societal expectation of privacy in the sum of one's public movements. I would ask whether people reasonably expect that their movements will be recorded and aggregated in a manner that enables the Government to ascertain, more or less at will, their political and religious beliefs, sexual habits, and so on. I do not regard as dispositive the fact that the Government might obtain the fruits of GPS monitoring through lawful conventional surveillance techniques. I would also consider the appropriateness of entrusting to the Executive, in the absence of any oversight from a coordinate branch, a tool so amenable to misuse, especially in light of the Fourth Amendment's goal to curb arbitrary exercises of police power [to] and prevent "a too permeating police surveillance."

More fundamentally, it may be necessary to reconsider the premise that an individual has no reasonable expectation of privacy in information voluntarily disclosed to third parties. This approach is ill suited to the digital age, in which people reveal a great deal of information about themselves to third parties in the course of carrying out mundane tasks. People disclose the phone numbers that they dial or text to their cellular providers; the URLs that they visit and the e-mail addresses with which they correspond to their Internet service providers; and the books, groceries, and medications they purchase to online retailers. Perhaps, as Justice ALITO notes, some people may find the "tradeoff" of privacy for convenience "worthwhile," or come to accept this "diminution of privacy" as "inevitable," and perhaps not. I for one doubt that people would accept without complaint the warrantless disclosure to the Government of a list of every Web site they had visited in the last week, or month, or year. But whatever the societal expectations, they can attain constitutionally protected status only if our Fourth Amendment jurisprudence ceases to treat secrecy as a prerequisite for privacy. I would not assume that all information voluntarily disclosed to some member of the public for a limited purpose is, for that reason alone, disentitled to Fourth Amendment protection.

Resolution of these difficult questions in this case is unnecessary, however, because the Government's physical intrusion on Jones' Jeep supplies a narrower basis for decision. I therefore join the majority's opinion.

Florida v. Jardines
133 S.Ct. 1409 (2013)

In 2006, William Pedraja of the Miami–Dade Police Department received an unverified tip that marijuana was being grown in the home of Joelis Jardines. One month later, the Department and the Drug Enforcement Administration sent a team to Jardines' home. Detective Pedraja watched the home for fifteen minutes and saw no vehicles in the driveway or activity around the home and could not see inside because the blinds were drawn. He then approached Jardines' home accompanied by detective Douglas Bartelt, a trained canine handler who had arrived with his drug-sniffing dog. Detective Bartelt had the dog on a six-foot leash, owing in part to the dog's "wild" nature and tendency to dart around erratically. As the dog approached Jardines' front porch, he apparently sensed one of the odors he had been trained to detect and began energetically exploring the area for the strongest point source of that odor. After sniffing the base of the front door, the dog sat—the trained behavior upon discovering the odor's strongest point—and Bartelt pulled the dog away from the door and returned to his vehicle. He then left after informing Pedraja that there had been a positive alert for narcotics. On the basis of what he had learned, Pedraja got a warrant to search the residence. When the warrant was executed later that day, Jardines was arrested and a search revealed marijuana plants. Subsequently, he was charged with trafficking in cannabis. At trial, Jardines moved to suppress the marijuana plants on the ground that the canine investigation was an unreasonable search. The trial court granted the motion, but a state appellate court reversed. On appeal the Florida Supreme Court held that the use of the trained narcotics dog was a Fourth Amendment search unsupported by probable cause, rendering invalid the warrant based upon information gathered in that search.

The Supreme Court granted review and affirmed the state supreme court's decision by a five-to-four vote. Justice Scalia delivered the opinion of the Court. Justice Kagan filed a concurring opinion, joined by Justices Ginsburg and Sotomayor. Justice Alito filed a dissenting opinion, which Chief Justice Roberts and Justices Kennedy and Breyer joined.

☐ *Justice SCALIA, delivered the opinion of the Court.*

The Fourth Amendment provides in relevant part that the "right of the people to be secure in their persons, houses, papers, and effects, against unreasonable searches and seizures, shall not be violated." The Amendment establishes a simple baseline, one that for much of our history formed the exclusive basis for its protections: When "the Government obtains information by physically intruding" on persons, houses, papers, or effects, "a 'search' within the original meaning of the Fourth Amendment" has "undoubtedly occurred." *United States v. Jones* (2012). By reason of our decision in *Katz v. United States*, 389 U.S. 276 (1967), property rights "are not the sole measure of Fourth Amendment"—but though *Katz* may add to the baseline, it does not subtract anything from the Amendment's protections "when the Government does engage in [a] physical intrusion of a constitutionally protected area," *United States v. Knotts*, 460 U.S. 276 (1983).

That principle renders this case a straightforward one. The officers were gathering information in an area belonging to Jardines and immediately surrounding his house—in the curtilage of the house, which we have held enjoys protection as part of the home itself. And they gathered that information by physically entering and occupying the area to engage in conduct not explicitly or implicitly permitted by the homeowner.

The Fourth Amendment "indicates with some precision the places and things encompassed by its protections": persons, houses, papers, and effects. *Oliver v. United States*, 466 U.S. 170 (1984). The Fourth Amendment does not, therefore, prevent all investigations conducted on private property; for example, an officer may (subject to *Katz*) gather information in what we have called "open fields"—even if those fields are privately owned—because such fields are not enumerated in the Amendment's text. *Hester v. United States*, 265 U.S. 57 (1924).

But when it comes to the Fourth Amendment, the home is first among equals. At the Amendment's "very core" stands "the right of a man to retreat into his own home and there be free from unreasonable governmental intrusion." *Silverman v. United States*, 365 U.S. 505 (1961). This right would be of little practical value if the State's agents could stand in a home's porch or side garden and trawl for evidence with impunity; the right to retreat would be significantly diminished if the police could enter a man's property to observe his repose from just outside the front window.

We therefore regard the area "immediately surrounding and associated with the home"—what our cases call the curtilage—as "part of the home itself for Fourth Amendment purposes." That principle has ancient and durable roots. Just as the distinction between the home and the open fields is "as old as the common law," *Hester*, so too is the identity of home and what Blackstone called the "curtilage or homestall," for the "house protects and privileges all its branches and appurtenants." This area around the home is "intimately linked to the home, both physically and psychologically," and is where "privacy expectations are most heightened." *California v. Ciraolo*, 476 U.S. 207 (1986).

While the boundaries of the curtilage are generally "clearly marked," the "conception defining the curtilage" is at any rate familiar enough that it is "easily understood from our daily experience." Here there is no doubt that the officers entered it: The front porch is the classic exemplar of an area adjacent to the home and "to which the activity of home life extends."

Since the officers' investigation took place in a constitutionally protected area, we turn to the question of whether it was accomplished through an unlicensed physical intrusion. While law enforcement officers need not "shield their eyes" when passing by the home "on public thoroughfares," an officer's leave to gather information is sharply circumscribed when he steps off those thoroughfares and enters the Fourth Amendment's protected areas. In permitting, for example, visual observation of the home from "public navigable airspace," we were careful to note that it was done "in a physically nonintrusive manner." *Entick v. Carrington*, 95 Eng. Rep. 807 (K. B. 1765), a case "undoubtedly familiar" to "every American statesman" at the time of the Founding, *Boyd v. United States*, 116 U.S. 616 (1886), states the general rule clearly: "[O]ur law holds the property of every man so sacred, that no man can set his foot upon his neighbour's close without his leave." As it is undisputed that the detectives had all four of their feet and all four of their companion's firmly planted on the constitutionally protected extension of Jardines' home, the only question is whether he had given his leave (even implicitly) for them to do so. He had not. . . .

[And] introducing a trained police dog to explore the area around the home in hopes of discovering incriminating evidence is something else. There is no customary invitation to do that. An invitation to engage in canine forensic investigation assuredly does not inhere in the very act of hanging a knocker. To find a visitor knocking on the door is routine (even if sometimes unwelcome); to spot that same visitor exploring the front path with a metal detector, or marching his bloodhound into the garden before saying hello and asking permission, would inspire most of us to—well, call the police. The scope of a license—express or implied—is limited not only to a particular area but also to a specific purpose. Consent at a traffic stop to an officer's checking out an anonymous tip that there is a body in the trunk does not permit the officer to rummage through the trunk for narcotics. Here, the background social norms that invite a visitor to the front door do not invite him there to conduct a search. . . .

The State argues that investigation by a forensic narcotics dog by definition cannot implicate any legitimate privacy interest. The State cites for authority our decisions in *United States v. Place*, 462 U.S. 696 (1983), *United States v. Jacobsen*, 466 U.S. 109 (1984), and *Illinois v. Caballes*, 543 U.S. 405 (2005), which held, respectively, that canine inspection of luggage in an airport, chemical testing of a substance that had fallen from a parcel in transit, and canine inspection of an automobile during a lawful traffic stop, do not violate the "reasonable expectation of privacy" described in *Katz*.

Just last Term, we considered an argument much like this. [*United States v.*] *Jones* [131 S.Ct. 945 (2012)] held that tracking an automobile's whereabouts using a physically-mounted GPS receiver is a Fourth Amendment search. The Government argued that the *Katz* standard "show[ed] that no search occurred," as the defendant had "no 'reasonable expectation of privacy'"—a proposition with at least as much support in our case law as the one the State marshals here. But because the GPS receiver had been physically mounted on the defendant's automobile (thus intruding on his "effects"), we held that tracking the vehicle's movements was a search: a person's "rights do not rise or fall with the *Katz* formulation." The *Katz* reasonable-expectations test "has been added to, not substituted for," the traditional property-based understanding of the Fourth Amendment, and so is unnecessary to consider when the government gains evidence by physically intruding on constitutionally protected areas.

Thus, we need not decide whether the officers' investigation of Jardines' home violated his expectation of privacy under *Katz*. One virtue of the Fourth Amendment's property-rights baseline is that it keeps easy cases easy. That the officers learned what they learned only by physically intruding on Jardines' property to gather evidence is enough to establish that a search occurred.

For a related reason we find irrelevant the State's argument (echoed by the dissent) that forensic dogs have been commonly used by police for centuries. This argument is apparently directed to our holding in *Kyllo v. United States*, 533 U.S. 27 (2001), that surveillance of the home is a search where "the Government uses a device that is not in general public use" to "explore details of the home that would previously have been unknowable without physical intrusion." But the implication of that statement is that when the government uses a physical intrusion to explore details of the home (including its curtilage), the antiquity of the tools that they bring along is irrelevant.

The government's use of trained police dogs to investigate the home and its immediate surroundings is a "search" within the meaning of the Fourth Amendment. The judgment of the Supreme Court of Florida is therefore affirmed.

□ *Justice KAGAN, with whom Justice GINSBURG, Justice SOTOMAYOR join, concurring.*

For me, a simple analogy clinches this case—and does so on privacy as well as property grounds. A stranger comes to the front door of your home carrying super-high-powered binoculars. He doesn't knock or say hello. Instead, he stands on the porch and uses the binoculars to peer through your windows, into your home's furthest corners. It doesn't take long (the binoculars are really very fine): In just a couple of minutes, his uncommon behavior allows him to learn details of your life you disclose to no one. Has your "visitor" trespassed on your property, exceeding the license you have granted to members of the public to, say, drop off the mail or distribute campaign flyers? Yes, he has. And has he also invaded your "reasonable expectation of privacy," by nosing into intimacies you sensibly thought protected from disclosure? *Katz v. United States* (1967) (HARLAN, J., concurring). Yes, of course, he has done that too. . . .

The Court today treats this case under a property rubric; I write separately to note that I could just as happily have decided it by looking to Jardines' privacy interests. A decision along those lines would have looked . . . well, much like this one. It would have talked about "'the right of a man to retreat into his own home and there be free from unreasonable governmental intrusion.'" It would have insisted on maintaining the "practical value" of that right by preventing police officers from standing in an adjacent space and "trawl[ing] for evidence with impunity." It would have explained that "'privacy expectations are most heightened'" in the home and the surrounding area. And it would have determined that police officers invade those shared expectations when they use trained canine assistants to reveal within the confines of a home what they could not otherwise have found there.

It is not surprising that in a case involving a search of a home, property concepts and privacy concepts should so align. The law of property "naturally enough influence[s]" our "shared social expectations" of what places should be free from governmental incursions. And so the sentiment "my home is my own," while originating in property law, now also denotes a common understanding—extending even beyond that law's formal protections—about an especially private sphere. Jardines' home was his property; it was also his most intimate and familiar space. The analysis proceeding from each of those facts, as today's decision reveals, runs mostly along the same path.

I can think of only one divergence: If we had decided this case on privacy grounds, we would have realized that *Kyllo v. United States*, 533 U.S. 27 (2001), already resolved it. The *Kyllo* Court held that police officers conducted a search when they used a thermal imaging device to detect heat emanating from a private home, even though they committed no trespass. Highlighting our intention to draw both a "firm" and a "bright" line at "the entrance to the house," we announced the following rule: "Where, as here, the Government uses a device that is not in general public use, to explore details of the home that would previously have been unknowable without physical intrusion, the surveillance is a 'search' and is presumptively unreasonable without a warrant."

That "firm" and "bright" rule governs this case: The police officers here conducted a search because they used a "device . . . not in general public use" (a trained drug-detection dog) to "explore details of the home" (the presence of certain substances) that they would not otherwise have discovered without entering the premises. . . .

☐ *Justice ALITO, with whom THE CHIEF JUSTICE, Justice KENNEDY, and Justice BREYER join, dissenting.*

The Court's decision in this important Fourth Amendment case is based on a putative rule of trespass law that is nowhere to be found in the annals of Anglo-American jurisprudence.

The law of trespass generally gives members of the public a license to use a walkway to approach the front door of a house and to remain there for a brief time. This license is not limited to persons who intend to speak to an occupant or who actually do so. (Mail carriers and persons delivering packages and flyers are examples of individuals who may lawfully approach a front door without intending to converse.) Nor is the license restricted to categories of visitors whom an occupant of the dwelling is likely to welcome; as the Court acknowledges, this license applies even to "solicitors, hawkers and peddlers of all kinds." And the license even extends to police officers who wish to gather evidence against an occupant (by asking potentially incriminating questions).

According to the Court, however, the police officer in this case, Detective Bartelt, committed a trespass because he was accompanied during his otherwise lawful visit to the front door of respondent's house by his dog, Franky. Where is the authority evidencing such a rule? Dogs have been domesticated for about 12,000 years; they were ubiquitous in both this country and Britain at the time of the adoption of the Fourth Amendment; and their acute sense of smell has been used in law enforcement for centuries. Yet the Court has been unable to find a single case—from the United States or any other common-law nation—that supports the rule on which its decision is based. Thus, trespass law provides no support for the Court's holding today.

The Court's decision is also inconsistent with the reasonable-expectations-of-privacy test that the Court adopted in *Katz v. United States*. A reasonable person understands that odors emanating from a house may be detected from locations that are open to the public, and a reasonable person will not count on the strength of those odors remaining within the range that, while detectible by a dog, cannot be smelled by a human.

For these reasons, I would hold that no search within the meaning of the Fourth Amendment took place in this case, and I would reverse the decision below. . . .

Contrary to the interpretation propounded by the concurrence, *Kyllo* is best understood as a decision about the use of new technology. The *Kyllo* Court focused on the fact that the thermal imaging device was a form of "sense-enhancing technology" that was "not in general public use," and it expressed concern that citizens would be "at the mercy of advancing technology" if its use was not restricted. A dog, however, is not a new form of "technology" or a "device." And, as noted, the use of dogs' acute sense of smell in law enforcement dates back many centuries.

The concurrence suggests that a *Kyllo*-based decision would be "much like" the actual decision of the Court, but that is simply not so. The holding of the Court is based on what the Court sees as a "'physical intrusion of a constitutionally protected area.'" As a result, it does not apply when a dog alerts while on a public sidewalk or street or in the corridor of a building to which the dog and handler have been lawfully admitted.

The concurrence's *Kyllo*-based approach would have a much wider reach. When the police used the thermal imaging device in *Kyllo*, they were on a public street and "committed no trespass." Therefore, if a dog's nose is just like a thermal imaging device for Fourth Amendment purposes, a search would occur if a dog alerted while on a public sidewalk or in the corridor of an apartment building. And the same would be true if the dog was trained to sniff, not for marijuana, but for more dangerous quarry, such as explosives or for a violent fugitive or kidnaped child. I see no ground for hampering legitimate law enforcement in this way.

The conduct of the police officer in this case did not constitute a trespass and did not violate respondent's reasonable expectations of privacy. I would hold that this conduct was not a search, and I therefore respectfully dissent.

B | *Exceptions to the Fourth Amendment Warrant Requirement*

In its 2011–2012 term the Court held that the Fourth Amendment was not violated by the strip search of an individual, who was arrested for a minor offense, when jailed, even though there was no reasonable suspicion that he possessed contraband or was dangerous, in *Florence v. Board of Chosen Freeholders*, 132 S.Ct. 1510 (2012). A New Jersey state trooper had stopped a car in which Albert Florence was a passenger and arrested him on the basis of an outstanding warrant. Florence contested the validity of the warrant but was taken to the Burlington county jail, where he was subjected to the jail's routine strip and body cavity search. He was held for six days, was transferred to another correctional facility, and underwent another strip search. The following day, the charges against him were dismissed. Subsequently, Florence sued, contending that his Fourth Amendment rights had been violated. Writing for the majority, Justice Kennedy deemed the jail's search procedures for all inmates was reasonable in balancing the needs of correctional facilities and inmates' privacy and that the creation of an exception for nonviolent offenders would be unworkable. Correction officials have significant interests in conducting thorough searches of new inmates in order to minimize risks to staff and to guard against the introduction of drugs and weapons, as well as to prevent gang violence. Justice Breyer, joined by Justices Ginsburg, Sotomayor, and Kagan, dissented. The Court had previously upheld the strip search of pretrial detainees in federal correctional facilities in order to discover and deter the smuggling of drugs and weapons in *Bell v. Wolfish*, 441 U.S. 520 (1979).

By an eight-to-one vote the Roberts Court expanded the "exigencies of the circumstances" exception to the requirement for a warrant for a search and seizure of property (see Vol. 2, Ch. 7) by approving a warrantless search and seizure based on "a police-created exigency" to justify a warrantless search because evidence might be destroyed so long as police do not "engag[e] or threaten[] to engage in conduct that violates the Fourth Amendment." In adopting that rule the Court rejected alternative tests, such as whether police acted in "bad faith" because that test turns on subjective motives. A test of "reasonable foreseeability" of the destruction of evidence was dismissed as too unpredictable, while drawing a line at whether police had time to obtain a warrant and didn't was deemed too restrictive. Under the new test, police could knock on a door and if they hear or see evidence being destroyed inside, their entry would be permissible. By contrast, police may not break down a door if the person inside won't open the door, since that violates the Fourth Amendment. Justice Alito delivered the opinion of the Court in *Kentucky v. King* (2011) (excerpted below), and Justice Ginsburg dissented.

However, by a six-to-three vote the Court limited the ruling in *Michigan v. Summers*, 452 U.S. 962 (1981), which held that police when executing a search warrant may "detain the occupants of the premises while a proper search is conducted." That ruling was further qualified and clarified in *Bailey v. United States*, 133 S.Ct. 1031 (2013), in holding that the *Summers* rule was limited to the immediate vicinity of the premises. In *Bailey*, police followed and detained Chunon Bailey about one mile from an apartment, where narcotics were found in plain view, and then arrested him. Justices Breyer, Thomas, and Alito dissented.

In its 2012–2013 term the Court also limited the "exigencies of circumstances" exception to the warrant requirement and rejected a per se rule that police have drivers suspected of driving under the influence of alcohol (DUI) submit to a blood test without their consent or a warrant; about half of the states require a warrant for DUI suspects. Tyler McNeely was stopped by a police officer for speeding and crossing the centerline. After declining to take a breath test to measure his blood alcohol concentration, he was arrested and taken to a nearby hospital for blood testing. The officer never attempted to secure a search warrant. McNeely refused to consent to the blood test, but the officer directed a lab technician to take a sample. McNeely tested well above the legal limit, and he was charged with driving while intoxicated. He moved to suppress the blood test result, arguing that taking his blood without a warrant violated his Fourth Amendment rights. The trial court agreed, concluding that the exigency exception to the warrant requirement did not apply because, apart from the fact that McNeely's blood alcohol was dissipating, no circumstances suggested that the officer faced an emergency. The Missouri Supreme Court affirmed, relying on *Schmerber v. California*, 384 U.S. 757 (1966), in which the Court upheld a DWI suspect's warrantless blood test where the officer "might reasonably have believed that he was confronted with an emergency, in which the delay necessary to obtain a warrant, under the circumstances, threatened 'the destruction of evidence.'" This case, the state court found, involved a routine DWI investigation where no factors other than the natural dissipation of blood alcohol suggested that there was an emergency, and, thus, the nonconsensual warrantless test violated McNeely's right to be free from unreasonable searches of his person. Writing for the Court in *Missouri v. McNeely*, 133 S.Ct. 1552 (2013), Justice Sotomayor affirmed and concluded that in drunk-driving investigations, the natural dissipation of alcohol in the bloodstream does not constitute an exigency in every case to justify a warrantless blood test. Justice Sotomayor held that only in exceptional circumstances may warrantless blood tests be conducted and that should be determined on a case-by-case basis based on "the totality of circumstances." In her words: "cases will arise when anticipated delays in obtaining a warrant will justify a blood test without judicial authorization. . . . [But our decision that consent or warrants must generally be obtained underscores] our recognition that any compelled intrusion into the human body implicates significant, constitutionally protected privacy interests." Chief Justice Roberts, joined by Justices Breyer and Alito, concurred and dissented in part, criticizing the vagueness of the majority's ruling with the observation that "A police officer reading this Court's opinion would [have] no idea— no idea—what the Fourth Amendment requires of him, once he decides to obtain a blood sample from a drunk-driving suspect who has refused a breathalyzer test." Only dissenting Justice Thomas would permit warrantless blood tests of drivers suspected of DWI.

Kentucky v. King
131 S.Ct. 1849 (2011)

Justice Alito's opinion for the Court and Justice Ginsburg's dissent discuss the facts of the case and reach very different results. The Kentucky Supreme Court had held that evidence obtained in a warrantless search should be excluded because police could have obtained a warrant but instead conducted a warrantless search based on "a foreseeable exigency" of the possible destruction of contraband. That court's decision was reversed by an eight-to-one vote.

☐ *Justice ALITO delivered the opinion of the Court.*

It is well established that "exigent circumstances," including the need to prevent the destruction of evidence, permit police officers to conduct an otherwise permissible search without first obtaining a warrant. In this case, we consider whether this rule applies when police, by knocking on the door of a residence and announcing their presence, cause the occupants to attempt to destroy evidence. The Kentucky Supreme Court held that the exigent circumstances rule does not apply in the case at hand because the police should have foreseen that their conduct would prompt the occupants to attempt to destroy evidence. We reject this interpretation of the exigent circumstances rule. The conduct of the police prior to their entry into the apartment was entirely lawful. They did not violate the Fourth Amendment or threaten to do so. In such a situation, the exigent circumstances rule applies.

This case concerns the search of an apartment in Lexington, Kentucky. Police officers set up a controlled buy of crack cocaine outside an apartment complex. Undercover Officer Gibbons watched the deal take place from an unmarked car in a nearby parking lot. After the deal occurred, Gibbons radioed uniformed officers to move in on the suspect. He told the officers that the suspect was moving quickly toward the breezeway of an apartment building, and he urged them to "hurry up and get there" before the suspect entered an apartment.

In response to the radio alert, the uniformed officers drove into the nearby parking lot, left their vehicles, and ran to the breezeway. Just as they entered the breezeway, they heard a door shut and detected a very strong odor of burnt marijuana. At the end of the breezeway, the officers saw two apartments, one on the left and one on the right, and they did not know which apartment the suspect had entered. Gibbons had radioed that the suspect was running into the apartment on the right, but the officers did not hear this statement because they had already left their vehicles. Because they smelled marijuana smoke emanating from the apartment on the left, they approached the door of that apartment.

Officer Steven Cobb, one of the uniformed officers who approached the door, testified that the officers banged on the left apartment door "as loud as [they] could" and announced, "'This is the police'" or "'Police, police, police.'" Cobb said that "[a]s soon as [the officers] started banging on the door," they "could hear people inside moving," and "[i]t sounded as [though] things were being moved inside the apartment." These noises, Cobb testified, led the officers to believe that drug-related evidence was about to be destroyed.

At that point, the officers announced that they "were going to make entry inside the apartment." Cobb then kicked in the door, the officers entered the apartment, and they found three people in the front room: respondent Hollis King, respondent's girlfriend, and a guest who was smoking marijuana. The officers performed a protective sweep of the apartment during which they saw marijuana and powder cocaine in plain view. In a subsequent search, they also discovered crack cocaine, cash, and drug paraphernalia.

Police eventually entered the apartment on the right. Inside, they found the suspected drug dealer who was the initial target of their investigation. [King was subsequently tried, convicted, and sentenced] to 11 years' imprisonment.

The Kentucky Court of Appeals affirmed. It held that exigent circumstances justified the warrantless entry because the police reasonably believed that evidence would be destroyed. The police did not impermissibly create the exigency, the court explained, because they did not deliberately evade the warrant requirement. The Supreme Court of Kentucky reversed. . . .

The text of the Amendment . . . expressly imposes two requirements. First, all searches and seizures must be reasonable. Second, a warrant may not be issued unless probable cause is properly established and the scope of the authorized search is set out with particularity. See *Payton v. New York*, 445 U.S. 573 (1980).

Although the text of the Fourth Amendment does not specify when a search warrant must be obtained, this Court has inferred that a warrant must generally be secured. "It is a 'basic principle of Fourth Amendment law,'" we have often said, "'that searches and seizures inside a home without a warrant are presumptively unreasonable.'" *Brigham City v. Stuart*, 547 U.S. 398 (2006). But we have also recognized that this presumption may be overcome in some circumstances because "[t]he ultimate touchstone of the Fourth Amendment is 'reasonableness.'" Accordingly, the warrant requirement is subject to certain reasonable exceptions.

One well-recognized exception applies when "'the exigencies of the situation' make the needs of law enforcement so compelling that [a] warrantless search is objectively reasonable under the Fourth Amendment." *Mincey v. Arizona*, 437 U.S. 385 (1978).

This Court has identified several exigencies that may justify a warrantless search of a home. Under the "emergency aid" exception, for example, "officers may enter a home without a warrant to render emergency assistance to an injured occupant or to protect an occupant from imminent injury." Police officers may enter premises without a warrant when they are in hot pursuit of a fleeing suspect. See *United States v. Santana*, 427 U.S. 38 (1976). And— what is relevant here—the need "to prevent the imminent destruction of evidence" has long been recognized as a sufficient justification for a warrantless search. *Brigham City*.

Over the years, lower courts have developed an exception to the exigent circumstances rule, the so-called "police-created exigency" doctrine. Under this doctrine, police may not rely on the need to prevent destruction of evidence when that exigency was "created" or "manufactured" by the conduct of the police. . . .

Despite the welter of tests devised by the lower courts, the answer to the question presented in this case follows directly and clearly from the principle that permits warrantless searches in the first place. As previously noted, warrantless searches are allowed when the circumstances make it reasonable, within the meaning of the Fourth Amendment, to dispense with the warrant requirement. Therefore, the answer to the question before us is that the exigent circumstances rule justifies a warrantless search when the conduct of the police preceding the exigency is reasonable in the same sense. Where, as here, the police did not create the exigency by engaging or threatening to engage in conduct that violates the Fourth Amendment, warrantless entry to prevent the destruction of evidence is reasonable and thus allowed. . . .

For these reasons, we conclude that the exigent circumstances rule applies when the police do not gain entry to premises by means of an actual or threatened violation of the Fourth Amendment. This holding provides ample protection for the privacy rights that the Amendment protects. . . .

☐ *Justice GINSBURG, dissenting*

This case involves a principal exception to the warrant requirement, the exception applicable in "exigent circumstances." "[C]arefully delineated," the exception should govern only in genuine emergency situations. Circumstances qualify as "exigent" when there is an imminent risk of death or serious injury, or danger that evidence will be immediately destroyed, or that a suspect will escape. The question presented: May police, who could pause to gain the approval of a neutral magistrate, dispense with the need to get a warrant by themselves creating exigent circumstances? I would answer no, as did the Kentucky Supreme Court. The urgency must exist, I would rule, when the police come on the scene, not subsequent to their arrival, prompted by their own conduct. . . .

Under an appropriately reined-in "emergency" or "exigent circumstances" exception, the result in this case should not be in doubt. The target of the investigation's entry into the building, and the smell of marijuana seeping under the apartment door into the hallway, the Kentucky Supreme Court rightly determined, gave the police "probable cause . . . sufficient . . . to obtain a warrant to search the . . . apartment." As that court observed, nothing made it impracticable for the police to post officers on the premises while proceeding to obtain a warrant authorizing their entry. . . .

C | *The Special Problems of Automobiles in a Mobile Society*

In its 2012–2013 term the Roberts Court decided *Florida v. Harris* 133 S.Ct. 1050 (2013), involving the use of drug-sniffing dogs in searches of automobiles. After stopping Harris for driving with expired tags, a police officer asked him for permission to search the vehicle. When Harris refused, the officer retrieved Aldo, a highly trained and certified narcotics detection dog. The dog sniffed the driver's door handle and indicated the presence of narcotics. And a search revealed all of the materials necessary to make methamphetamine but no actual narcotics. The trial court denied a motion to suppress evidence due to an illegal search and found that there was probable cause to support a search of the vehicle; an appellate court affirmed. But the Florida Supreme Court reversed, holding that evidence that a dog has been trained and certified to detect narcotics was insufficient on its own to establish the dog's reliability for purposes of determining probable cause. Florida appealed that decision and the Supreme Court granted *certiorari* to address whether a canine sniff is sufficient to establish probable cause upon a showing that the dog was properly trained and certified to detect drugs, or whether additional evidence of the dog's proficiency is required. The state contended that its state supreme court's decision ran counter to *Illinois v. Caballes*, 543 U.S. 405 (2005), which held that police may use drug-sniffing dogs around a car stopped for a routine traffic violation and that evidence of contraband discovered as a result may be used at trial. In addition, the state argues that dog training and certification is enough to establish probable cause and the alert on sniffing the residual odor on the car door does not undermine that certification. Moreover, the state claims that its supreme court improperly expanded the definition of a "well-trained drug dog."

The Supreme Court unanimously reversed the Florida Supreme Court. In an opinion for the Court, Justice Kagan held: "The question—similar to every inquiry into probable cause—is whether all the facts surrounding a dog's alert, viewed through the lens of common sense, would make a reasonably prudent person think that a search would reveal contraband or evidence of a crime. . . . A sniff is up to snuff when it meets that test. . . . Aldo's did."

F | *The Exclusionary Rule*

A solid majority of the Roberts Court held that warrantless searches of cars incident to an arrest of occupants made with reasonable reliance on binding precedents do not trigger the exclusionary rule, even if the kind of search conducted is later found to violate the Fourth Amendment. Writing for the Court in *Davis v. United States* (2011) (excerpted below), Justice Alito's opinion swept broadly with regard to "good faith" exceptions to the exclusionary rule and with respect to the retroactivity to pending cases of new rulings on impermissible searches and seizures. Notably, the majority expressly held that the exclusionary rule is merely a judicially created remedy and not a principle commanded by the Fourth Amendment. Justices Ginsburg and Breyer dissented.

Davis v. United States
131 S.Ct. 2419 (2011)

In Greenville, Alabama, Willie Davis was arrested by police during a routine vehicle stop for giving a false name. The police searched the car and found a revolver. Davis was arrested, tried and convicted for being a felon in possession of a firearm. At trial, his attorney moved to exclude the evidence, even though he knew that it complied with existing precedents. While Davis's appeal was pending, the Supreme Court announced a new rule on automobile searches incident to arrests of occupants, in *Arizona v. Gant*, 129 S.Ct. 1710 (2009). A panel of the Court of Appeals for the Eleventh Circuit held that, under *Gant*, the vehicle search in his case violated the Fourth Amendment but declined to suppress the evidence and affirmed Davis's conviction. That decision was appealed and granted review.

The appellate court's decision was affirmed by a seven-to-two vote. Justice Alito delivered the opinion for the Court. Justice Sotomayor filed a concurring opinion. Justice Breyer filed a dissenting opinion, which Justice Ginsburg joined.

☐ *JUSTICE ALITO delivered the opinion of the Court.*

The question here is whether to apply [the exclusionary rule] when the police conduct a search in compliance with binding precedent that is later overruled. Because suppression would do nothing to deter police misconduct in these circumstances, and because it would come at a high cost to both the truth and the public safety, we hold that searches conducted in objectively reasonable reliance on binding appellate precedent are not subject to the exclusionary rule.

The question presented arises in this case as a result of a shift in our Fourth Amendment jurisprudence on searches of automobiles incident to arrests of recent occupants.

Under this Court's decision in *Chimel v. California*, 395 U.S. 752 (1969), a police officer who makes a lawful arrest may conduct a warrantless search of the arrestee's person and the area "within his immediate control." This rule "may be stated clearly enough," but in the early going after *Chimel* it proved difficult to apply, particularly in cases that involved searches "inside [of] automobile[s] after the arrestees [we]re no longer in [them]." See *New York v. Belton*, 453 U.S. 454 (1981). . . .

In *Belton*, a police officer conducting a traffic stop lawfully arrested four occupants of a vehicle and ordered the arrestees to line up, un-handcuffed, along the side of the thruway. The officer then searched the vehicle's passenger compartment and found cocaine inside a jacket that lay on the backseat. This Court upheld the search as reasonable incident to the occupants' arrests. In an opinion that repeatedly stressed the need for a "straightforward," "workable rule" to guide police conduct, the Court announced "that when a policeman has made a lawful custodial arrest of the occupant of an automobile, he may, as a contemporaneous incident of that arrest, search the passenger compartment of that automobile."

For years, *Belton* was widely understood to have set down a simple, bright-line rule. . . .

Not every court, however, agreed with this reading of *Belton*. In *State v. Gant*, the Arizona Supreme Court considered an automobile search conducted after the vehicle's occupant had been arrested, handcuffed, and locked in a patrol car. The court distinguished *Belton* as a case in which "four unsecured" arrestees "presented an immediate risk of loss of evidence and an obvious threat to [a] lone officer's safety." The court held that where no such "exigencies exis[t]"—where the arrestee has been subdued and the scene secured—the rule of *Belton* does not apply.

This Court granted *certiorari* in *Gant* and affirmed in a 5-to-4 decision. *Arizona v. Gant*, [129 S.Ct. 1710] (2009). Four of the Justices in the majority agreed with the Arizona Supreme Court that *Belton*'s holding applies only where "the arrestee is unsecured and within reaching distance of the passenger compartment at the time of the search." The four dissenting Justices, by contrast, understood *Belton* to have explicitly adopted the simple, bright-line rule stated in the *Belton* Court's opinion. Justice SCALIA, who provided the fifth vote to affirm in *Gant*, agreed with the dissenters' understanding of *Belton*'s holding. Justice SCALIA favored a more explicit and complete overruling of *Belton*, but he joined what became the majority opinion to avoid "a 4-to-1-to-4" disposition. As a result, the Court adopted a new, two-part rule under which an automobile search incident to a recent occupant's arrest is constitutional (1) if the arrestee is within reaching distance of the vehicle during the search, or (2) if the police have reason to believe that the vehicle contains "evidence relevant to the crime of arrest."

The search at issue in this case took place a full two years before this Court announced its new rule in *Gant*. . . .

The Fourth Amendment protects the "right of the people to be secure in their persons, houses, papers, and effects, against unreasonable searches and seizures." The Amendment says nothing about suppressing evidence obtained in violation of this command. That rule—the exclusionary rule—is a "prudential" doctrine, *Pennsylvania Bd. of Probation and Parole v. Scott*, 524 U.S. 357 (1998), created by this Court to "compel respect for the constitutional guaranty." *Elkins v. United States*, 364 U.S. 206 (1960); see *Weeks v. United States*, 232 U.S. 383 (1914); *Mapp v. Ohio*, 367 U.S. 643 (1961). Exclusion is "not a personal constitutional right," nor is it designed to "redress the injury" occasioned by an unconstitutional search. *Stone v. Powell*, 428 U.S. 465 (1976). . . .

In time, however, we came to acknowledge the exclusionary rule for what it undoubtedly is—a "judicially created remedy" of this Court's own making. We abandoned the old, "reflexive" application of the doctrine, and imposed a more rigorous weighing of its costs and deterrence benefits. In a line of cases beginning with *United States v. Leon*, 468 U.S. 897 [(1984)], we also recalibrated our cost-benefit analysis in exclusion cases to focus the inquiry on the "flagrancy of the police misconduct" at issue. . . .

The question in this case is whether to apply the exclusionary rule when the police conduct a search in objectively reasonable reliance on binding judicial precedent. At the time of the search at issue here, we had not yet decided *Arizona v. Gant* and the Eleventh Circuit had interpreted our decision in *New York v. Belton*, 453 U.S. 454 [(1981)], to establish a bright-line rule authorizing the search of a vehicle's passenger compartment incident to a recent occupant's arrest. . . .

Under our exclusionary-rule precedents, this acknowledged absence of police culpability dooms Davis's claim. . . . Indeed, in 27 years of practice under *Leon*'s good-faith exception, we have "never applied" the exclusionary rule to suppress evidence obtained as a result of nonculpable, innocent police conduct. . . .

The principal argument of both the dissent and Davis is that the exclusionary rule's availability to enforce new Fourth Amendment precedent is a retroactivity issue, see *Griffith v. Kentucky*, 479 U.S. 314 (1987), not a good-faith issue. They contend that applying the good-faith exception where police have relied on overruled precedent effectively revives the discarded retroactivity regime of *Linkletter v. Walker*, 381 U.S. 618 (1965).

In *Linkletter*, we held that the retroactive effect of a new constitutional rule of criminal procedure should be determined on a case-by-case weighing of interests. For each new rule, *Linkletter* required courts to consider a three-factor balancing test that looked to the "purpose" of the new rule, "reliance" on the old rule by law enforcement and others, and the effect retroactivity would have "on the administration of justice." . . . In *Linkletter* itself, the balance of interests prompted this Court to conclude that *Mapp v. Ohio*, 367 U.S. 643 [(1961)]—which incorporated the exclusionary rule against the States—should not apply retroactively to cases already final on direct review.

Over time, *Linkletter* proved difficult to apply in a consistent, coherent way. Individual applications of the standard "produced strikingly divergent results" that many saw as "incompatible" and "inconsistent." . . . Eventually, and after more than 20 years of toil under *Linkletter*, the Court adopted Justice HARLAN's view and held that newly announced rules of constitutional criminal procedure must apply "retroactively to all cases, state or federal, pending on direct review or not yet final, with no exception." *Griffith* [*v. Kentucky*, 479 U.S. 314 (1987)].

Our retroactivity jurisprudence is concerned with whether, as a categorical matter, a new rule is available on direct review as a potential ground for relief. Retroactive application under *Griffith* lifts what would otherwise be a categorical bar to obtaining redress for the government's violation of a newly announced constitutional rule. . . .

When this Court announced its decision in *Gant*, Davis's conviction had not yet become final on direct review. *Gant* therefore applies retroactively to this case. Davis may invoke its newly announced rule of substantive Fourth Amendment law as a basis for seeking relief. The question, then, becomes one of remedy, and on that issue Davis seeks application of the exclusionary rule. But exclusion of evidence does not automatically follow from the fact that a Fourth Amendment violation occurred. The remedy is subject to exceptions and applies only where its "purpose is effectively advanced." . . .

It is true that, under the old retroactivity regime of *Linkletter*, the Court's decisions on the "retroactivity problem in the context of the exclusionary rule" did take into account whether "law enforcement officers reasonably believed in good faith" that their conduct was in compliance with governing law. As a matter of retroactivity analysis, that approach is no longer applicable. It does not follow, however, that reliance on binding precedent is irrelevant in applying the good-faith exception to the exclusionary rule. . . . That reasonable reliance by police was once a factor in our retroactivity cases does not make it any less relevant under our *Leon* line of cases.

It is one thing for the criminal "to go free because the constable has blundered." *People v. Defore*, 242 N.Y. 13 (1926) (CARDOZO, J.). It is quite another to set the criminal free because the constable has scrupulously adhered to governing law. Excluding evidence in such cases deters no police misconduct and imposes substantial social costs. We therefore hold that when the police conduct a search in objectively reasonable reliance on binding appellate precedent, the exclusionary rule does not apply.

□ *Justice BREYER, with whom Justice GINSBURG joins, dissenting.*

I agree with the Court about whether *Gant*'s new rule applies. . . . The Court goes on, however, to decide how *Gant*'s new rule will apply. And here it adds a fatal twist. While conceding that, like the search in *Gant*, this search violated the Fourth Amendment, it holds that, unlike *Gant*, this defendant is not entitled to a remedy. That is because the Court finds a new "good faith" exception which prevents application of the normal remedy for a Fourth Amendment violation, namely, suppression of the illegally seized evidence. Leaving Davis with a right but not a remedy, the Court "keep[s] the word of promise to our ear" but "break[s] it to our hope."

At this point I can no longer agree with the Court. A new "good faith" exception and this Court's retroactivity decisions are incompatible. For one thing, the Court's distinction between (1) retroactive application of a new rule and (2) availability of a remedy is highly artificial and runs counter to precedent. To determine that a new rule is retroactive is to determine that, at least in the normal case, there is a remedy. As we have previously said, the "source of a 'new rule' is the Constitution itself, not any judicial power to create new rules of law"; hence, "[w]hat we are actually determining when we assess the 'retroactivity' of a new rule is not the temporal scope of a newly announced right, but whether a violation of the right that occurred prior to the announcement of the new rule will entitle a criminal defendant to the relief sought." The Court's "good faith" exception (unlike, say, inevitable discovery, a remedial doctrine that applies only upon occasion) creates "a categorical bar to obtaining redress" in every case pending when a precedent is overturned.

For another thing, the Court's holding re-creates the very problems that led the Court to abandon *Linkletter*'s approach to retroactivity in favor of *Griffith*'s. One such problem concerns workability. The Court says that its exception applies where there is "objectively reasonable" police "reliance on binding appellate precedent." But to apply the term "binding appellate precedent" often requires resolution of complex questions of degree. . . .

Another such problem concerns fairness. Today's holding, like that in *Linkletter*, "violates basic norms of constitutional adjudication." It treats the defendant in a case announcing a new rule one way while treating similarly situated defendants whose cases are pending on appeal in a different way. . . .

If the Court means what it says, what will happen to the exclusionary rule, a rule that the Court adopted nearly a century ago for federal courts, *Weeks v. United States*, and made applicable to state courts a half century ago through the Fourteenth Amendment, *Mapp v. Ohio*? The Court has thought of that rule not as punishment for the individual officer or as reparation for the individual defendant but more generally as an effective way to secure enforcement of the Fourth Amendment's commands. This Court has deviated from the "suppression" norm in the name of "good faith" only a handful of times and in limited, atypical circumstances: where a magistrate has erroneously issued a warrant, *United States v. Leon*, 468 U.S. 897 (1984); where a database has erroneously informed police that they have a warrant, *Arizona v. Evans*, 514 U.S. 1 (1995), *Herring v. United States*, 555 U.S. 135 (2009); and where an unconstitutional statute purported to authorize the search, *Illinois v. Krull*, 480 U.S. 340 (1987). . . .

In sum, I fear that the Court's opinion will undermine the exclusionary rule. And I believe that the Court wrongly departs from *Griffith* regardless. Instead I would follow *Griffith*, apply *Gant*'s rule retroactively to this case, and require suppression of the evidence. Such an approach is consistent with our precedent, and it would indeed affect no more than "an exceedingly small set of cases."

For these reasons, with respect, I dissent.

8

The Fifth Amendment Guarantee against Self-Accusation

A | Coerced Confessions and Police Interrogations

In its 2010–2011 term a bare majority of the Court held that in determining whether minors are in "police custody," for the purposes of triggering the requirement of giving *Miranda* warnings of the right to remain silent, their age may be taken into consideration, in *J. D. B. v. North Carolina* (2011) (excerpted below). At issue was the police questioning and the confession of a thirteen-year-old at school. Justice Alito, joined by Chief Justice Roberts and Justices Scalia and Thomas, dissented, contending that the majority was departing from *Miranda*'s "bright-line rule" on when an individual becomes a "suspect" and reverting to the older "totality of circumstances" rule for determining coerced confessions.

In *Howes v. Fields*, 132 S.Ct. 1181 (2012) (in THE DEVELOPMENT OF LAW box below), however, the Court further weakened the *Miranda* ruling. There, the majority now joined Justice Alito in holding that courts in determining whether a person is in "custody," and thus entitled to *Miranda* warnings, should consider "all of the circumstances surrounding the interrogation" when determining whether a prisoner is in "custody" for *Miranda* purposes. In *Miranda* the Court observed that "the very fact of custodial interrogation exacts a heavy toll on individual liberty, and trades on the weaknesses of individuals." But *Howes v. Fields* held that courts should consider how an interrogated prisoner would have gauged his or her freedom of movement and that not all restraints on freedom of movement amount to *Miranda* custody. Randall Fields, a prisoner, was taken from his prison cell and questioned by two sheriffs about criminal activities prior to going to prison. At no time was he given *Miranda* warnings or advised that he had a right to remain silent. During more than five hours of questioning, he was told that he could return to his cell and several times said that he no longer wanted to speak to the deputies but never asked to return to his cell. Fields eventually confessed and that confession was used against him at trial.

The following term also writing for the Court, in *Salinas v. Texas*, 133 S.Ct. 2174 (2013), Justice Alito held that prosecutors may comment at trial on a defendant's unwillingness to respond to an officer's questions about a murder, even as a suspect he had not yet been arrested or taken into custody and without receiving *Miranda* warnings. In doing so, Justice Alito distinguished *Griffin v. California*, 380 U.S. 609 (1965), and other precedents supporting the right to remain silent, because here the individual had not invoked the Fifth Amendment privilege against self-incrimination. Concurring justices would have overturned *Griffin* as inconsistent with "the Constitution's text, history, or logic." By contrast, dissenting Justice Breyer, joined by Justices Ginsburg, Sotomayor, and Kagan, countered that the ruling was inconsistent with a range of precedents as well as *Miranda* and the Fifth Amendment guarantee. In Justice Breyer's words: "The Fifth Amendment prohibits prosecutors from commenting on an individual's silence where that silence amounts to an effort to avoid becoming 'a witness against himself.' This Court has specified that 'a rule of evidence' permitting 'commen[t] . . . by counsel' in a criminal case upon a defendant's failure to testify 'violates the Fifth Amendment.' *Griffin*."

J. D. B. v. North Carolina
131 S.Ct. 2394 (2011)

Justice Sotomayor discusses the facts in this case in her opinion for the Court. Justice Alito filed a dissenting opinion, joined by Chief Justice Roberts and Justices Scalia and Thomas.

□ *Justice SOTOMAYOR delivered the opinion of the Court.*

This case presents the question whether the age of a child subjected to police questioning is relevant to the custody analysis of *Miranda v. Arizona*, 384 U.S. 436 (1966). It is beyond dispute that children will often feel bound to submit to police questioning when an adult in the same circumstances would feel free to leave. Seeing no reason for police officers or courts to blind themselves to that commonsense reality, we hold that a child's age properly informs the *Miranda* custody analysis.

Petitioner J. D. B. was a 13-year-old, seventh-grade student attending class at Smith Middle School in Chapel Hill, North Carolina when he was removed from his classroom by a uniformed police officer, escorted to a closed-door conference room, and questioned by police for at least half an hour.

This was the second time that police questioned J. D. B. in the span of a week. Five days earlier, two home break-ins occurred, and various items were stolen. Police stopped and questioned J. D. B. after he was seen behind a residence in the neighborhood where the crimes occurred. That same day, police also spoke to J. D. B.'s grandmother—his legal guardian—as well as his aunt.

Police later learned that a digital camera matching the description of one of the stolen items had been found at J. D. B.'s middle school and seen in J. D. B.'s possession. Investigator DiCostanzo, the juvenile investigator with the local police force who had been assigned to the case, went to the school to question J. D. B. Upon arrival, DiCostanzo informed the uniformed police officer on detail to the school (a so-called school resource officer), the assistant principal, and an administrative intern that he was there to question J. D. B. about the break-ins. . . .

Questioning began with small talk—discussion of sports and J. D. B.'s family life. DiCostanzo asked, and J. D. B. agreed, to discuss the events of the prior weekend. Denying any wrongdoing, J. D. B. explained that he had been in the neighborhood where the crimes occurred because he was seeking work mowing lawns. DiCostanzo pressed J. D. B. for additional detail about his efforts to obtain work; asked J. D. B. to explain a prior incident, when one of the victims returned home to find J. D. B. behind her house; and confronted J. D. B. with the stolen camera. The assistant principal urged J. D. B. to "do the right thing," warning J. D. B. that "the truth always comes out in the end."

Eventually, J. D. B. asked whether he would "still be in trouble" if he returned the "stuff." In response, DiCostanzo explained that return of the stolen items would be helpful, but "this thing is going to court" regardless. DiCostanzo then warned that he may need to seek a secure custody order if he believed that J. D. B. would continue to break into other homes. When J. D. B. asked what a secure custody order was, DiCostanzo explained that "it's where you get sent to juvenile detention before court."

After learning of the prospect of juvenile detention, J. D. B. confessed that he and a friend were responsible for the break-ins. DiCostanzo only then informed J. D. B. that he could refuse to answer the investigator's questions and that he was free to leave. Asked whether he understood, J. D. B. nodded and provided further detail, including information about the location of the stolen items. Eventually J. D. B. wrote a statement, at DiCostanzo's request. When the bell rang indicating the end of the school day, J. D. B. was allowed to leave to catch the bus home. . . .

We granted *certiorari* to determine whether the *Miranda* custody analysis includes consideration of a juvenile suspect's age. . . .

By its very nature, custodial police interrogation entails "inherently compelling pressures." *Miranda.* . . . Recognizing that the inherently coercive nature of custodial interrogation "blurs the line between voluntary and involuntary statements," *Dickerson* [*v. United States*, 530 U.S. 428 (2000)], this Court in *Miranda* adopted a set of prophylactic measures designed to safeguard the constitutional guarantee against self-incrimination. . . .

Because these measures protect the individual against the coercive nature of custodial interrogation, they are required "only where there has been such a restriction on a person's freedom as to render him 'in custody.'" *Stansbury v. California*, 511 U.S. 318 (1994). As we have repeatedly emphasized, whether a suspect is "in custody" is an objective inquiry. "Two discrete inquiries are essential to the determination: first, what were the circumstances surrounding the interrogation; and second, given those circumstances, would a reasonable person have felt he or she was at liberty to terminate the interrogation and leave. Once the scene is set and the players' lines and actions are reconstructed, the court must apply an objective test to resolve the ultimate inquiry: was there a formal arrest or restraint on freedom of movement of the degree associated with formal arrest." *Thompson v. Keohane*, 516 U.S. 99 (1995). Rather than demarcate a limited set of relevant circumstances, we have required police officers and courts to "examine all of the circumstances surrounding the interrogation," including any circumstance that "would have affected how a reasonable person" in the suspect's position "would perceive his or her freedom to leave." On the other hand, the "subjective views harbored by either the interrogating officers or the person being questioned" are irrelevant. The test, in other words, involves no consideration of the "actual mindset" of the particular suspect subjected to police questioning. . . .

The State and its *amici* contend that a child's age has no place in the custody analysis, no matter how young the child subjected to police questioning. We cannot agree. . . . a child's age differs from other personal characteristics that, even when known to police, have no objectively discernible relationship to a reasonable person's understanding of his freedom of action. . . .

[W]e hold that so long as the child's age was known to the officer at the time of police questioning, or would have been objectively apparent to a reasonable officer, its inclusion in the custody analysis is consistent with the objective nature of that test. This is not to say that a child's age will be a determinative, or even a significant, factor in every case. It is, however, a reality that courts cannot simply ignore. . . .

□ *Justice ALITO, with whom THE CHIEF JUSTICE, Justice SCALIA, and Justice THOMAS join, dissenting.*

The Court's decision in this case may seem on first consideration to be modest and sensible, but in truth it is neither. It is fundamentally inconsistent with one of the main justifications for the *Miranda* rule: the perceived need for a clear rule that can be easily applied in all cases. And today's holding is not needed to protect the constitutional rights of minors who are questioned by the police. . . .

Today's decision shifts the *Miranda* custody determination from a one-size-fits-all reasonable-person test into an inquiry that must account for at least one individualized characteristic—age—that is thought to correlate with susceptibility to coercive pressures. Age, however, is in no way the only personal characteristic that may correlate with pliability, and in future cases the Court will be forced to choose between two unpalatable alternatives. It may choose to limit today's decision by arbitrarily distinguishing a suspect's age from other personal characteristics—such as intelligence, education, occupation, or prior experience with law enforcement—that may also correlate with susceptibility to coercive pressures. Or, if the Court is unwilling to draw these arbitrary lines, it will be forced to effect a fundamental transformation of the *Miranda* custody test—from a clear, easily applied prophylactic rule into a highly fact-intensive standard resembling the voluntariness test that the *Miranda* Court found to be unsatisfactory.

For at least three reasons, there is no need to go down this road. First, many minors subjected to police interrogation are near the age of majority, and for these suspects the one-size-fits-all *Miranda* custody rule may not be a bad fit. Second, many of the difficulties in applying the *Miranda* custody rule to minors arise because of the unique circumstances present when the police conduct interrogations at school. The *Miranda* custody rule has always taken into account the setting in which questioning occurs, and accounting for the school setting in such cases will address many of these problems. Third, in cases like the one now before us, where the suspect is especially young, courts applying the constitutional voluntariness standard can take special care to ensure that incriminating statements were not obtained through coercion. . . .

I respectfully dissent.

■ THE DEVELOPMENT OF LAW

Other Rulings on Coerced Confessions and Limiting Miranda

CASE	VOTE	RULING
Howes v. Fields, 132 S.Ct. 1181 (2012)	6:3	Writing for the Court, Justice Alito held that in determining when a prisoner is in custody for

Miranda purposes, courts should consider "all of the circumstances surrounding the interrogation," specifically how a suspect would have gauged his freedom of movement, and that not all restraints on freedom of movement amount to custody. Fields, a prisoner, was taken from his prison cell and questioned by two sheriffs about criminal activities prior to going to prison. At no time was he given *Miranda* warnings. Although during more than five hours of questioning he was told that he could return to his cell and several times said he no longer wanted to talk, he never asked to return to his cell. Fields eventually confessed and that confession was used against him at trial. Justices Ginsburg, Breyer, and Sotomayor concurred and dissented in part.

Salinas v. Texas, 133 S.Ct. 2174 (2013)	5:4	Justice Alito held that prosecutors may comment at trial on a defendants unwillingness to respond to

an officer's questions about a murder, even as a suspect he had not yet been arrested or taken into custody and without receiving *Miranda* warnings. In doing so, Justice Alito distinguished *Griffin v. California,* 380 U.S. 609 (1965), and other precedents supporting the right to remain silent, because here the individual had not invoked the Fifth Amendment privilege against self-incrimination. Concurring Justices would have overturned *Griffin* as inconsistent with "the Constitution's text, history, or logic." By contrast, dissenting Justice Breyer, joined by Justices Ginsburg, Sotomayor, and Kagan, countered that the ruling was inconsistent with a range of precedents, as well as *Miranda* and the Fifth Amendment guarantee.

C | *Real versus Testimonial Evidence*

In *Missouri v. McNeely*, 132 S.Ct. 1552 (2013), the Court clarified and qualified its ruling in *Schmerber v. California*, 384 U.S. 757 (1966), on the taking of blood samples from drivers suspected of driving under the influence of alcohol. Tyler McNeely was stopped by a police officer for speeding and crossing the centerline. After declining to take a breath test to measure his blood alcohol concentration, he was arrested and taken to a nearby hospital for blood testing. The officer never attempted to secure a search warrant. McNeely refused to consent to the blood test, but the officer directed a lab technician to take a sample. McNeely tested well above the legal limit, and he was charged with driving while intoxicated (DUI). He moved to suppress the blood test result, arguing that taking his blood without a warrant violated his Fourth Amendment rights. The trial court agreed, concluding that the exigency exception to the warrant requirement did not apply because, apart from the fact that McNeely's blood alcohol was dissipating, no circumstances suggested that the officer faced an emergency. The Missouri Supreme Court affirmed, relying on *Schmerber v. California*, in which the Court upheld a DUI suspect's warrantless blood test where the officer "might reasonably have believed that he was confronted with an emergency, in which the delay necessary to obtain a warrant, under the circumstances, threatened 'the destruction of evidence.'" This case, the state court found, involved a routine DWI investigation where no factors other than the natural dissipation of blood alcohol suggested that there was an emergency, and, thus, the nonconsensual warrantless test violated McNeely's right to be free from unreasonable searches of his person. Writing for the Court, Justice Sotomayor affirmed and concluded that in drunk-driving investigations, the natural dissipation of alcohol in the bloodstream does constitute an exigency in every case to justify a warrantless blood test. Justice Sotomayor held that only in exceptional circumstances may warrantless blood tests be conducted and that should be determined on a case-by-case basis based on "the totality of circumstances." In her words: "cases will arise when anticipated delays in obtaining a warrant will justify a blood test without judicial authorization. . . . [But our decision that consent or warrants must generally be obtained underscores] our recognition that any compelled intrusion into the human body implicates significant, constitutionally protected privacy interests." Chief Justice Roberts, joined by Justices Breyer and Alito, concurred and dissented in part, while dissenting Justice Thomas would permit warrantless blood tests of drivers suspected of DWI.

■ THE DEVELOPMENT OF LAW

Other Rulings on Real versus Testimonial Evidence

CASE	VOTE	RULING
Maryland v. King, 133 S.Ct. 1958 (2013)	5:4	The majority held that the police may take DNA swabs from suspects arrested (but not yet tried

and convicted) for "serious" violent crimes. Writing for the Court, Justice Kennedy likened the DNA samples to fingerprinting during a suspect's booking as "a safe and secure way to process and identify the persons and possessions they must take into custody." By contrast, dissenting Justice Scalia, joined by Justices Ginsburg, Sotomayor, and Kagan, countered that the DNA swabs amounted to a general search warrant in order to possibly solve "cold cases" and thus lacked reasonable individualized suspicion. Alonzo Jay King Jr. was arrested for assault and police took a DNA sample that ultimately linked him to a six-year-old unresolved rape case, for which he was subsequently tried, convicted, and sentenced to life imprisonment.

9

THE RIGHT TO COUNSEL AND OTHER PROCEDURAL GUARANTEES

A | The Right to Counsel

■ THE DEVELOPMENT OF LAW

Rulings Extending the Right to Counsel throughout the Criminal Justice System

	CASES
Plea Bargaining	*Missouri v. Frye*, 132 S.Ct. 1399 (2012), and *Lafler v. Cooper*, 132 U.S. 1376 (2012)

B | Plea Bargaining and the Right to Effective Counsel

In two landmark rulings on the Sixth Amendment right to counsel, a bare majority of the Roberts Court ruled that the accused has a right to effective counsel with respect to plea bargains. In both cases, Justice Kennedy wrote for the majority and Chief Justice Roberts and Justices Scalia, Thomas, and Alito dissented. In *Missouri v. Frye* (2012) (excerpted below) the Court held that "the constitutional right to counsel extends to the negotiation and consideration of plea offers that lapse or are rejected" and that defendants must show that prejudice due to ineffective counsel—based on "a reasonable probability they would have accepted the earlier plea offer had they been afforded effective counsel" and "a reasonable probability the plea would have been entered without the prosecution canceling it or the trial court refusing to accept it." In doing so, Justice Kennedy emphasized that "[c]riminal justice today is for the most part a system of pleas, not a system of trials," in light of the fact that 97 percent of convictions in federal courts and 94 percent in state courts are the result of plea bargains. In a companion ruling, *Lafler v. Cooper*, 132 S.Ct. 1376 (2012), involving a different context of a defendant's attorney reporting a favorable plea offer but recommending a rejection of the offer that resulted in a trial and a harsher sentence than would have been obtained by agreeing to a plea bargain.

In such circumstances, Justice Kennedy held that "a defendant must show that but for the ineffective advice of counsel there is a reasonable probability that the plea offer would have been presented to the court," that the court would have accepted its terms, and that the conviction or sentence, or both, under the offer's terms would have been less severe than under the judgment and sentence that in fact were imposed." In addition, *Lafler* held that the appropriate remedy must "neutralize the taint" of the constitutional violation but not provide a "windfall" to the defendant. In some situations the trial court may conduct an evidentiary hearing and exercise its discretion in resentencing the defendant. In other situations, Justice Kennedy suggested, "the prosecution [might] reoffer the plea proposal. Once this has occurred, the judge can then exercise discretion in deciding whether to vacate the conviction from trial and accept the plea or leave the conviction undisturbed." For the dissenters, Justice Scalia complained that the majority's ruling was inconsistent with precedents and invited "a whole new field of constitutionalized criminal procedure: plea-bargaining law."

Missouri v. Frye
131 S.Ct. 1399 (2012)

Galin Frye was charged with driving with a revoked license and, because he had three other convictions for the same offense, he was charged

with a felony carrying a maximum four-year prison sentence. The prosecutor offered Frye's counsel two possible plea bargains, including one to
reduce the charge to a misdemeanor and to recommend a 90-day sentence. The attorney, however, failed to tell Frye about the offers and they
expired. Less than a week before his preliminary hearing, Frye was again
arrested for driving with a revoked license. He subsequently pleaded guilty
without a plea agreement and was sentenced to three years in prison.
But on appeal, Frye alleged that his attorney's failure to inform him of
the plea offers deprived him of his Sixth Amendment right to the effective assistance of counsel, and testified that he would have pleaded guilty
to the misdemeanor had he known of the offer. The trial court denied
his motion but the Missouri appellate court reversed, holding that Frye
met both of the requirements for showing a Sixth Amendment violation under *Strickland v. Washington*, 466 U.S. 668 (1984). That court found
that Frye's counsel was ineffective in not communicating the plea offers
to him and concluded that he had shown that counsel's deficient performance caused prejudice because he pleaded guilty to a felony instead
of a misdemeanor. The state appealed that decision.

Justice Kennedy delivered the opinion of the Court. Justice Scalia
filed a dissenting opinion, joined by Chief Justice Roberts and Justices
Thomas and Alito.

□ *Justice KENNEDY delivered the opinion of the Court.*

The right to counsel is the right to effective assistance of counsel. See *Strickland v. Washington*, 466 U.S. 668 (1984). This case arises in the context of claimed
ineffective assistance that led to the lapse of a prosecution offer of a plea bargain, a proposal that offered terms more lenient than the terms of the guilty
plea entered later. The initial question is whether the constitutional right to
counsel extends to the negotiation and consideration of plea offers that lapse
or are rejected. If there is a right to effective assistance with respect to those
offers, a further question is what a defendant must demonstrate in order to
show that prejudice resulted from counsel's deficient performance. Other questions relating to ineffective assistance with respect to plea offers, including the
question of proper remedies, are considered in a second case decided today.
See *Lafler v. Cooper*, [132 S.Ct. 1376 (2012)]. . . .

It is well settled that the right to the effective assistance of counsel applies to certain steps before trial. Critical stages include arraignments, postindictment interrogations, postindictment lineups, and the entry of a guilty plea.

With respect to the right to effective counsel in plea negotiations, a proper
beginning point is to discuss two cases from this Court considering the role of
counsel in advising a client about a plea offer and an ensuing guilty plea: *Hill
v. Lockhart*, 474 U.S. 52 (1985); and *Padilla v. Kentucky*, [132 S.Ct. 1473] (2010).

Hill established that claims of ineffective assistance of counsel in the plea
bargain context are governed by the two-part test set forth in *Strickland*.
[T]he Missouri Court of Appeals, applying the two-part test of *Strickland*,
determined first that defense counsel had been ineffective and second that
there was resulting prejudice.

In *Hill*, the decision turned on the second part of the *Strickland* test. There, a defendant who had entered a guilty plea claimed his counsel had misinformed him of the amount of time he would have to serve before he became eligible for parole. But the defendant had not alleged that, even if adequate advice and assistance had been given, he would have elected to plead not guilty and proceed to trial. Thus, the Court found that no prejudice from the inadequate advice had been shown or alleged.

In *Padilla*, the Court again discussed the duties of counsel in advising a client with respect to a plea offer that leads to a guilty plea. Padilla held that a guilty plea, based on a plea offer, should be set aside because counsel misinformed the defendant of the immigration consequences of the conviction. The Court made clear that "the negotiation of a plea bargain is a critical phase of litigation for purposes of the Sixth Amendment right to effective assistance of counsel." It also rejected the argument made by petitioner in this case that a knowing and voluntary plea supersedes errors by defense counsel.

In the case now before the Court the State, as petitioner, points out that the legal question presented is different from that in *Hill* and *Padilla*. In those cases the claim was that the prisoner's plea of guilty was invalid because counsel had provided incorrect advice pertinent to the plea. In the instant case, by contrast, the guilty plea that was accepted, and the plea proceedings concerning it in court, were all based on accurate advice and information from counsel. The challenge is not to the advice pertaining to the plea that was accepted but rather to the course of legal representation that preceded it with respect to other potential pleas and plea offers. . . .

The State is correct to point out that *Hill* and *Padilla* concerned whether there was ineffective assistance leading to acceptance of a plea offer, a process involving a formal court appearance with the defendant and all counsel present. Before a guilty plea is entered the defendant's understanding of the plea and its consequences can be established on the record. This affords the State substantial protection against later claims that the plea was the result of inadequate advice. . . .

When a plea offer has lapsed or been rejected, however, no formal court proceedings are involved. This underscores that the plea-bargaining process is often in flux, with no clear standards or timelines and with no judicial supervision of the discussions between prosecution and defense. Indeed, discussions between client and defense counsel are privileged. . . .

Ninety-seven percent of federal convictions and ninety-four percent of state convictions are the result of guilty pleas. The reality is that plea bargains have become so central to the administration of the criminal justice system that defense counsel have responsibilities in the plea bargain process, responsibilities that must be met to render the adequate assistance of counsel that the Sixth Amendment requires in the criminal process at critical stages. Because ours "is for the most part a system of pleas, not a system of trials," *Lafler*, it is insufficient simply to point to the guarantee of a fair trial as a backstop that inoculates any errors in the pretrial process. In today's criminal justice system, therefore, the negotiation of a plea bargain, rather than the unfolding of a trial, is almost always the critical point for a defendant. . . .

The inquiry then becomes how to define the duty and responsibilities of defense counsel in the plea bargain process. This is a difficult question. Bargaining is, by its nature, defined to a substantial degree by personal style. The alternative courses and tactics in negotiation are so individual that it may be neither prudent nor practicable to try to elaborate or define detailed standards for the proper discharge of defense counsel's participation in the process.

Here the question is whether defense counsel has the duty to communicate the terms of a formal offer to accept a plea on terms and conditions that may result in a lesser sentence, a conviction on lesser charges, or both.

This Court now holds that, as a general rule, defense counsel has the duty to communicate formal offers from the prosecution to accept a plea on terms and conditions that may be favorable to the accused. Any exceptions to that rule need not be explored here, for the offer was a formal one with a fixed expiration date. When defense counsel allowed the offer to expire without advising the defendant or allowing him to consider it, defense counsel did not render the effective assistance the Constitution requires.

Here defense counsel did not communicate the formal offers to the defendant. As a result of that deficient performance, the offers lapsed. Under *Strickland*, the question then becomes what, if any, prejudice resulted from the breach of duty.

To show prejudice from ineffective assistance of counsel where a plea offer has lapsed or been rejected because of counsel's deficient performance, defendants must demonstrate a reasonable probability they would have accepted the earlier plea offer had they been afforded effective assistance of counsel. Defendants must also demonstrate a reasonable probability the plea would have been entered without the prosecution canceling it or the trial court refusing to accept it, if they had the authority to exercise that discretion under state law. To establish prejudice in this instance, it is necessary to show a reasonable probability that the end result of the criminal process would have been more favorable by reason of a plea to a lesser charge or a sentence of less prison time. . . .

In order to complete a showing of *Strickland* prejudice, defendants who have shown a reasonable probability they would have accepted the earlier plea offer must also show that, if the prosecution had the discretion to cancel it or if the trial court had the discretion to refuse to accept it, there is a reasonable probability neither the prosecution nor the trial court would have prevented the offer from being accepted or implemented. This further showing is of particular importance because a defendant has no right to be offered a plea, nor a federal right that the judge accept it. . . .

These standards must be applied to the instant case. As regards the deficient performance prong of *Strickland*, the Court of Appeals found the "record is void of any evidence of any effort by trial counsel to communicate the [formal] Offer to Frye during the Offer window, let alone any evidence that Frye's conduct interfered with trial counsel's ability to do so." On this record, it is evident that Frye's attorney did not make a meaningful attempt to inform the defendant of a written plea offer before the offer expired. The Missouri Court of Appeals was correct that "counsel's representation fell below an objective standard of reasonableness."

The Court of Appeals erred, however, in articulating the precise standard for prejudice in this context. As noted, a defendant in Frye's position must show not only a reasonable probability that he would have accepted the lapsed plea but also a reasonable probability that the prosecution would have adhered to the agreement and that it would have been accepted by the trial court. Frye can show he would have accepted the offer, but there is strong reason to doubt the prosecution and the trial court would have permitted the plea bargain to become final.

There appears to be a reasonable probability Frye would have accepted the prosecutor's original offer of a plea bargain if the offer had been communicated to him, because he pleaded guilty to a more serious charge, with no promise of a sentencing recommendation from the prosecutor. . . .

The Court of Appeals failed, however, to require Frye to show that the first plea offer, if accepted by Frye, would have been adhered to by the prosecution and accepted by the trial court. Whether the prosecution and trial court are required to do so is a matter of state law, and it is not the place of this Court to settle those matters. The Court has established the minimum requirements of the Sixth Amendment as interpreted in *Strickland*, and States have the discretion to add procedural protections under state law if they choose. A State may choose to preclude the prosecution from withdrawing a plea offer once it has been accepted or perhaps to preclude a trial court from rejecting a plea bargain. . . .

☐ *Justice SCALIA, with whom THE CHIEF JUSTICE, Justice THOMAS, and Justice ALITO join, dissenting.*

Counsel's mistake did not deprive Frye of any substantive or procedural right; only of the opportunity to accept a plea bargain to which he had no entitlement in the first place. So little entitlement that, had he known of and accepted the bargain, the prosecution would have been able to withdraw it right up to the point that his guilty plea pursuant to the bargain was accepted. . . .

While the inadequacy of counsel's performance in this case is clear enough, whether it was prejudicial (in the sense that the Court's new version of *Strickland* requires) is not. The Court's description of how that question is to be answered on remand is alone enough to show how unwise it is to constitutionalize the plea-bargaining process. Prejudice is to be determined, the Court tells us, by a process of retrospective crystal-ball gazing posing as legal analysis. First of all, of course, we must estimate whether the defendant would have accepted the earlier plea bargain. Here that seems an easy question, but as the Court acknowledges, it will not always be. Next, since Missouri, like other States, permits accepted plea offers to be withdrawn by the prosecution (a reality which alone should suffice, one would think, to demonstrate that Frye had no entitlement to the plea bargain), we must estimate whether the prosecution would have withdrawn the plea offer. And finally, we must estimate whether the trial court would have approved the plea agreement. These last two estimations may seem easy in the present case, since Frye committed a new infraction before the hearing at which the agreement would have been presented; but they assuredly will not be easy in the mine run of cases. . . .

The plea-bargaining process is a subject worthy of regulation, since it is the means by which most criminal convictions are obtained. It happens not to be, however, a subject covered by the Sixth Amendment, which is concerned not with the fairness of bargaining but with the fairness of conviction. "The Constitution . . . is not an all-purpose tool for judicial construction of a perfect world; and when we ignore its text in order to make it that, we often find ourselves swinging a sledge where a tack hammer is needed." *Padilla v. Kentucky* (2010) (SCALIA, J., dissenting). In this case and its companion, the Court's sledge may require the reversal of perfectly valid, eminently just, convictions. A legislature could solve the problems presented by these cases in a much more precise and efficient manner. It might begin, for example, by penalizing the attorneys who made such grievous errors. That type of sub-constitutional remedy is not available to the Court, which is limited to penalizing (almost) everyone else by reversing valid convictions or sentences. Because that result is inconsistent with the Sixth Amendment and decades of our precedent, I respectfully dissent.

D | The Right to an Impartial Jury Trial

The Court further extended its ruling in *Apprendi v. New Jersey*, 536 U.S. 466 (2000), that enhanced sentences (which go beyond mandatory sentencing guidelines) may be imposed only by juries (and not judges) to criminal fines as a penalty in *Southern Union Company v. United States*, 132 S.Ct. 2344 (2012).

A bare majority also overturned its decision in *Harris v. United States*, 536 U.S. 545 (2002), in which the Court had upheld judicial factfinding that increases a mandatory minimum sentence for a crime under the Sixth Amendment. Writing for the Court in *Alleyne v. United States*, 133 S.Ct. 2151 (2013), Justice Thomas held that *Harris* was inconsistent with *Apprendi* and the original meaning of the Sixth Amendment because here the jury had not decided the actual sentence, but rather the sentencing judge increased the sentence from five to seven years based on mandatory guidelines. Justice Thomas reaffirmed that the Sixth Amendment and *Apprendi* require juries to determine the facts beyond a reasonable doubt that justify a sentence. Chief Justice Roberts dissented and was joined by Justice Scalia and Kennedy; Justice Alito dissented in separate opinion.

F | The Right to Be Informed of Charges and to Confront Accusers

The Court continues to confront litigation over its ruling in *Crawford v. Washington*, 541 U.S. 36 (2004). There, writing for a unanimous Court, Justice Scalia ostensibly laid down a bright-line rule that the prosecution may use statements of an absent witness against the accused at trial only if they were previously cross-examined by the defense counsel at a deposition or in a prior trial. But since *Crawford* the Court has carved out some exceptions, dealing for example with the use of child abuse victims' statements against defendants, in balancing the Sixth Amendment's guarantee of defendants' right to confront witnesses and the introduction of hearsay evidence at trial (see Vol. 2, Ch. 9).

In its 2010–2011 term the Court dealt with Sixth Amendment confrontation claims in two cases. In *Michigan v. Bryant*, 131 S.Ct. 1143 (2011), a majority of the Court held that a dying victim's statements identifying the assailant could be introduced at trial against the defendant. Richard Bryant, who had been shot in a parking lot, identified his assailant to police investigating the crime scene and died shortly afterward. His statements were introduced at trial but held by the state supreme court to violate the Sixth Amendment and to run afoul of the ruling in *Crawford*. But writing for a majority, Justice Sotomayor distinguished the application of *Crawford*'s ruling and the statements here as "nontestimonial" because they were made to police at the time they were responding to "an ongoing emergency" and there was a "potential threat to the responding police and the public at large." By contrast, statements to police that amount to "testimony" about the accused are not allowed to be used at trial. Dissenting Justice Scalia, the author of the decision in *Crawford*, sharply rejected the majority's distinction between nontestimonial and testimonial in limiting the holding in *Crawford*. Justice Ginsburg also dissented, on separate grounds.

In a second decision, in *Bullcoming v. New Mexico*, 131 S.Ct. 2705 (2011), the Court confronted the issue of whether crime lab reports may be introduced as evidence against the defendant even though the author of the report is unavailable to testify against the defendant. Donald Bullcoming struck a car at a stop sign and was later alleged to have been driving under the influence of alcohol. After he left the crime scene, he allegedly went for drinks with friends, subsequently was located again by police, and failed a gas chromatograph test for blood alcohol content. The analyst who signed the forensic report was unavailable to testify at trial, and prosecutors called another analyst from the lab to testify. At issue, thus, was if a lab machine provides the incriminating evidence against the accused, does it matter which lab analyst testifies about the lab results and confronts the accused? Writing for a bare majority, Justice Ginsburg held that the Confrontation Clause does not permit the prosecution to introduce a forensic report, containing a testimonial certification, and call an analyst who did not conduct, observe, or certify the test reported. The accused right is to confront the analyst who made the certification and, if unavailable at trial, the accused must have an opportunity during a pretrial hearing to cross-examine that particular scientist.

In its 2011–2012 term the Court continued to limit the ruling in *Crawford*. A bare majority in *Williams v. Illinois*, 132 S.Ct. 2221 (2012), ruled that it was constitutionally permissible for an expert witness to discuss others' testimonial statements if they were not themselves admitted as evidence. Sandra Lambatos, a forensic specialist in the state police lab, testified that she matched a DNA profile produced by an outside laboratory, Cellmark, to a profile the state lab produced using a sample of the petitioner's blood. She offered no other statement for the purpose of identifying the sample used for Cellmark's profile or establishing how it tested the sample. The defense moved to exclude Lambatos's testimony, but the prosecution countered that the defendant's confrontation rights were satisfied because he had the opportunity to cross-examine the expert who had testified as to the match. The trial judge admitted the evidence and found the defendant guilty, which on appeal was affirmed by a state appellate and supreme court. The Supreme Court affirmed that decision. Justice Kagan dissented and was joined by Justices Scalia, Ginsburg, and Sotomayor. Justice Kagan contended that the majority was trying to apply an eighteenth-century conception of the right to confront one's accusers to twenty-first-century evidence such as DNA testing. Writing for a plurality, Justice Alito maintained that Lamatos's testimony about the lab report was not offered to prove that it was true and that Cellmark's report was not the sort of evidence to which the confrontation clause applies because it was made "for the purpose of finding a rapist who was on the loose." Justice Thomas cast the deciding vote and, disagreeing with Justice Alito's opinion for the Court, contended that "the confrontation clause . . . [applies] to a narrow class of statements bearing indicia of solemnity." But, Justice Kagan countered that "would turn the confrontation clause into a constitutional geegaw—nice for show, but of little value." In a concurring opinion, Justice Breyer advanced his consequentualist position that to rule otherwise and require lab analysts to testify would create enormous logistical problems for courts.

G | *The Guarantee against Double Jeopardy*

In *Blueford v. Arkansas*, 132 S.Ct. 2044 (2012), Chief Justice Roberts, writing for the majority, held that the Double Jeopardy Clause does not bar the retrial of the accused on charges of capital murder and first-degree murder after the jury in the original trial told the judge that it had voted unanimously against those charges but was deadlocked on a manslaughter charge and failed to reach a verdict, and the judge declared a mistrial. In other words, because the jury could not agree on all the charges, the judge could properly declare a mistrial, requiring a second trial on all the charges. Justice Sotomayor filed a dissenting opinion, which Justices Ginsburg and Kagan joined.

In *Evans v. Michigan*, 133 S.Ct. 1069 (2013), the Court, with only Justice Alito dissenting, held that the Double Jeopardy Clause bars a retrial after an acquittal even if the acquittal was erroneous.

IO

CRUEL AND UNUSUAL PUNISHMENT

In a controversial ruling in *Brown v. Plata*, 131 S.Ct. 1910 (2011), a bare majority of the Court affirmed a three-judge-court-issued injunction for the release of approximately 40,000 inmates in California's prison system due to overcrowding that created conditions of cruel and unusual punishment in violation of the Eighth Amendment. The system was designed to house about 80,000 but at various times held between 140,000 and more than 160,000 prisoners; and the lower court ordered a reduction of the prison population to 100,000. In affirming the lower court, the majority emphasized that, "As many as 200 prisoners may live in a gymnasium, monitored by as few as two or three correctional officers . . . [and that as] many as 54 prisoners may share a single toilet, as well as that about one prisoner per week commits suicide." Writing for the Court, Justice Kennedy acknowledged that, "The release of prisoners in large numbers—assuming the state finds no other way to comply with the order—is a matter of undoubted, grave concern." "Yet," he stressed, "so too is the continuing injury and harm resulting from these serious constitutional violations. . . . A prison that deprives prisoners of basic sustenance, including adequate medical care, is incompatible with the concept of human dignity and has no place in civilized society." In complying with the court's order, Justice Kennedy underscored that the state could achieve the reduction by a variety of means, including releasing the least dangerous convicts, transferring inmates to other prisons, and building more prisons. Justices Ginsburg, Breyer, Sotomayor, and Kagan joined his opinion.

By contrast, dissenting Justice Scalia, joined by Justice Thomas, blasted the majority for affirming "perhaps the most radical injunction issued by a court in our nation's history." They emphasized that courts exceed their authority and are ill equipped to bring about such major changes through "structural injunctions" and "institutional-reform litigation." In a separate dissent Justice Alito, joined by Chief Justice Roberts, lamented the inevitable impact on public safety: "I fear that today's decision, like prior prisoner-release orders, will lead to a grim roster of victims. I hope that I am wrong. In a few years, we will see."

Continuing a trend in the last couple of decades a bare majority of the Court struck down mandatory life sentences without the possibility of parole for juvenile murders in *Miller v. Alabama*, 132 S.Ct. 2455 (2012), invalidating a federal statute and mandatory-sentencing laws in 28 states. Writing for the Court, Justice Kagan held that "Mandatory life without parole for a juvenile precludes consideration of his chronological age and its hallmark features—among them, immaturity, impetuosity, and failure to appreciate risks and consequences . . . . It prevents taking into account the family and home environment that surrounds him—and from which he cannot usually extricate himself—no matter how brutal or dysfunctional." In doing so, the Court ruled that judges may still sentence juveniles convicted of murder to a life sentence without the possibility of parole but must take into consideration mitigating circumstances. Chief Justice Roberts and Justices Scalia, Thomas, and Alito dissented. Dissenting Justice Alito countered: "Even a 17 1/2-year-old who sets off a bomb in a crowded mall or guns down a dozen students and teachers is a 'child' and must be given a chance to persuade a judge to permit his release into society. . . . Nothing in the Constitution supports this arrogation of legislative authority." In a separate dissent, Chief Justice Roberts echoed that position, observing: "Determining the appropriate sentence for a teenager convicted of murder presents grave and challenging questions of morality and social policy [that legislatures should decide]. Our role, however, is to apply the law, not to answer such questions."

11

THE RIGHT OF PRIVACY

A | *Privacy and Reproductive Freedom*

In its 2013–2014 term, the Court will consider an appeal of the Oklahoma Supreme Court's decision striking down abortion regulations as
inconsistent with the ruling in *Planned Parenthood of Southeastern Pennsylvania v. Casey* (1992) (excerpted in Vol. 2, Ch. 11), in *Cline v. Oklahoma
Coalition for Reproductive Justice* (No. 12-1094). House Bill 1970 (HB
1970) amended Oklahoma's Public Health Code to require that abortion
inducing drugs be administered according to Food and Drug Administration (FDA) protocols. A group of reproductive health care providers
challenged the law, claiming that several provisions violated the state
constitution. A state district court found that Oklahoma's constitution
contained "a right to an abortion [that] was coextensive with the federal
right," and that HB 1970's purpose was to create a substantial obstacle
or "undue burden" under *Planned Parenthood of Southeastern Pennsylvania
v. Casey*. The Oklahoma Supreme Court held HB 1970 unconstitutional. The Supreme Court granted *certiorari* pending a response from
the state supreme court on whether HB 1970 prohibits (1) the use of
misoprostol to induce abortions, including the use of misoprostol in
conjunction with mifepristone according to a protocol approved by the
FDA; and (2) the use of methotrexate to treat ectopic pregnancies.

12

THE EQUAL PROTECTION OF THE LAWS

By a six-to-three vote in *Armour v. City of Indianapolis*, 132 S.Ct. 2073 (2012), the Court reaffirmed that legislatures have broad authority to create classifications in tax systems. In 2005 Indianapolis abandoned apportioning the cost of sewer projects to the owners of improved property and switched to a bond system. Prior to the switch, landowners had the option of paying a lump sum or paying the assessment in installments. When the change was made, landowners paying in installments were forgiven their debt. Christine Armour had paid the lump sum and sought a partial refund. When denied, she sued, claiming a violation of the equal protection of the law. Writing for the Court, Justice Breyer held that the city had a rational basis for distinguishing between lot owners who had already paid their assessments and those who had not. And the line the city chose to draw, distinguishing past payments from future obligations, did not violate the Fourteenth Amendment, which requires a rational (not a perfect) line; therefore, distinguishing between the two groups of taxpayers was not an equal protection violation. Chief Justice Roberts, joined by Justices Scalia and Alito, dissented.

C | *Affirmative Action and Reverse Discrimination*

In a widely watched challenge to the University of Texas at Austin's affirmative-action admissions program, the Court reaffirmed that achieving a diverse student body is a compelling governmental interest, as upheld in *Regents of the University of California v. Bakke*, 438 U.S. 265 (1978) (excerpted in Vol. 2, Ch. 12), and *Grutter v. Bollinger*, 539 U.S. 306 (2003) (excerpted in Vol. 2, Ch. 12). But writing for the Court in *Fisher v. University of Texas at Austin*, 133 S.Ct. 2411 (2013), Justice Kennedy ruled that the lower court failed to apply strict scrutiny and to ensure that the admissions policy was narrowly tailored. The University of Texas admitted about 75 percent of its students if they graduated in the top 10 percent of their high school class and thus achieved a measure of diversity since many of the state's high schools are dominated by one race or ethnicity. The remaining applicants were considered on a "holistic" basis—individual considerations such as legacy, special talents, and race or ethnicity. Abigail Fisher, a white woman, was not admitted and sued, claiming that the effort to increase the numbers of African Americans and Latinos cost her admission and violated the Fourteenth Amendment. While reaffirming that courts should give deference to universities' admission policies aimed at achieving diverse student bodies, Justice Kennedy ruled that "[t]*he reviewing court must ultimately be satisfied that no workable race-neutral alternatives would produce the educational benefits of diversity*" (emphasis added). In separate concurring opinions, Justices Scalia and Thomas indicated that they would have overruled *Grutter* but had not been asked to do so here. Dissenting Justice Ginsburg would have affirmed the lower court's analysis and upholding of the University of Texas's admissions program; Justice Kagan was recused from the decision.

In its 2013 term, the Roberts Court will consider another challenge to affirmative action in *Schuette v. Coalition to Defend Affirmative Action* (Docket No. 12-682). At issue is whether a state violates the Equal Protection Clause by amending its constitution to prohibit race- and sex-based discrimination or preferential treatment in public university admissions. In 2006 Michigan voters adopted an amendment to the state constitution. The so-called Proposal 2 amendment stated that no "public college could discriminate against, or grant preferential treatment to, any individual or group on the basis of race, sex, color, ethnicity, or national origin in the operation of public employment, public education, or public contracting." A federal district court rejected a challenge to the constitutionality of the amendment, but the Sixth Circuit Court of Appeals held that Proposal 2 violated the Equal Protection Clause. The appellate court held that Proposal 2 had a "racial focus" because it "inures primarily to the benefit of the minority." In addition, Proposal 2 was part of the "political process" and imposed a "special burden" on minorities. After finding that Proposal 2 failed that two-prong test, the appellate court applied the strict scrutiny test and found no compelling governmental interest and held Proposal 2 unconstitutional.

D | *Nonracial Classifications and the Equal Protection of the Laws*

(2) *Discrimination against Gays and Lesbians*

In two widely watched cases bearing on same-sex marriages, the Court split in different five-to-four rulings. On the one hand, in *Hollingsworth v. Perry* (2013) (excerpted in Vol. 1, Ch. 2), Chief Justice Roberts denied standing to sue to supporters of Proposition 8, a California state amendment barring same-sex marriages. Justice Kennedy, joined by Justices Thomas, Alito, and Sotomayor, dissented. On the other hand, in *United States v. Windsor* (2013) (excerpted below) Justice Kennedy struck down Section 3 of the Defense of Marriage Act of 1996, which denied federal benefits to same-sex couples. Chief Justice Roberts and Justices Scalia, Alito, and Thomas dissented.

Hollingsworth v. Perry
133 S.Ct. 2652 (2013)

(reprise, excerpted in Vol. 1, Ch. 2)

United States v. Windsor
133 S.Ct. 2675 (2013)

New York recognized the marriage of Edith Windsor and Thea Spyer, who wed in Ontario, Canada, in 2007. When Spyer died in 2009, she left her entire estate to Windsor. Windsor sought to claim the federal estate tax exemption for surviving spouses but was barred from doing so by Section 3 of the federal Defense of Marriage Act of 1996 (DOMA), which defined "marriage" and "spouse" as excluding same-sex partners. Windsor paid $363,053 in estate taxes and sought a refund, which the Internal Revenue Service denied. Windsor brought this refund suit, contending that DOMA violates the principles of equal protection incorporated in the Fifth Amendment. While the suit was pending, the attorney general notified the Speaker of the House of Representatives that the Department of Justice would no longer defend Section 3's constitutionality. In response, the Bipartisan Legal Advisory Group of the House of Representatives voted to intervene in the litigation to defend Section 3's constitutionality. A federal district court permitted the intervention and ruled against the United States, finding Section 3 unconstitutional and ordering the Treasury to refund Windsor's tax with interest. On appeal, the Supreme Court granted *certiorari* and struck down Section 3 of DOMA.

Justice Kennedy delivered the opinion of the Court. Chief Justice Roberts and Justices Scalia and Alito filed dissenting opinions. Justice Thomas joined parts of the latter's dissent.

☐ *Justice KENNEDY delivered the opinion of the Court.*

Section 3 of DOMA provides as follows: "In determining the meaning of any Act of Congress, or of any ruling, regulation, or interpretation of the various administrative bureaus and agencies of the United States, the word 'marriage' means only a legal union between one man and one woman as husband and wife, and the word 'spouse' refers only to a person of the opposite sex who is a husband or a wife."

The definitional provision does not by its terms forbid States from enacting laws permitting same-sex marriages or civil unions or providing state benefits to residents in that status. The enactment's comprehensive definition of marriage for purposes of all federal statutes and other regulations or directives covered by its terms, however, does control over 1,000 federal laws in which marital or spousal status is addressed as a matter of federal law. . . .

When at first Windsor and Spyer longed to marry, neither New York nor any other State granted them that right. After waiting some years, in 2007 they traveled to Ontario to be married there. It seems fair to conclude that, until recent years, many citizens had not even considered the possibility that two persons of the same sex might aspire to occupy the same status and dignity as that of a man and a woman in lawful marriage. For marriage between a man and a woman no doubt had been thought of by most people as essential to the very definition of that term and to its role and function throughout the history of civilization.

That belief, for many who long have held it, became even more urgent, more cherished when challenged. For others, however, came the beginnings of a new perspective, a new insight. Accordingly some States concluded that same-sex marriage ought to be given recognition and validity in the law for those same-sex couples who wish to define themselves by their commitment to each other. The limitation of lawful marriage to heterosexual couples, which for centuries had been deemed both necessary and fundamental, came to be seen in New York and certain other States as an unjust exclusion.

Slowly at first and then in rapid course, the laws of New York came to acknowledge the urgency of this issue for same-sex couples who wanted to affirm their commitment to one another before their children, their family, their friends, and their community. And so New York recognized same-sex marriages performed elsewhere; and then it later amended its own marriage laws to permit same-sex marriage. New York, in common with, as of this writing, 11 other States and the District of Columbia, decided that same-sex couples should have the right to marry and so live with pride in themselves and their union and in a status of equality with all other married persons. After a state-wide deliberative process that enabled its citizens to discuss and weigh arguments for and against same-sex marriage, New York acted to enlarge the definition of marriage to correct what its citizens and elected representatives perceived to be an injustice that they had not earlier known or understood.

Against this background of lawful same-sex marriage in some States, the design, purpose, and effect of DOMA should be considered as the beginning point in deciding whether it is valid under the Constitution. By history and tradition the definition and regulation of marriage, as will be discussed in more detail, has been treated as being within the authority and realm of the separate States. Yet it is further established that Congress, in enacting discrete statutes, can make determinations that bear on marital rights and privileges. Just this Term the Court upheld the authority of the Congress to preempt state laws, allowing a former spouse to retain life insurance proceeds under a federal program that gave her priority, because of formal beneficiary designation rules, over the wife by a second marriage who survived the husband. This is one example of the general principle that when the Federal Government acts in the exercise of its own proper authority, it has a wide choice of the mechanisms and means to adopt. Congress has the power both to ensure efficiency in the administration of its programs and to choose what larger goals and policies to pursue. . . .

In order to assess the validity of that intervention it is necessary to discuss the extent of the state power and authority over marriage as a matter of history and tradition. State laws defining and regulating marriage, of course, must respect the constitutional rights of persons, see, e.g., *Loving v. Virginia*, 388 U.S. 1 (1967); but, subject to those guarantees, "regulation of domestic relations" is "an area that has long been regarded as a virtually exclusive province of the States." *Sosna v. Iowa*, 419 U.S. 393, 404 (1975).

The recognition of civil marriages is central to state domestic relations law applicable to its residents and citizens. Consistent with this allocation of authority, the Federal Government, through our history, has deferred to state-law policy decisions with respect to domestic relations. Federal courts will not hear divorce and custody cases even if they arise in diversity because of "the virtually exclusive primacy . . . of the States in the regulation of domestic relations."

The significance of state responsibilities for the definition and regulation of marriage dates to the Nation's beginning; for "when the Constitution was adopted the common understanding was that the domestic relations of husband and wife and parent and child were matters reserved to the States." Marriage laws vary in some respects from State to State. For example, the required minimum age is 16 in Vermont, but only 13 in New Hampshire. Likewise the permissible degree of consanguinity can vary (most States permit first cousins to marry, but a handful—such as Iowa and Washington—prohibit the practice). But these rules are in every event consistent within each State.

Against this background DOMA rejects the long-established precept that the incidents, benefits, and obligations of marriage are uniform for all married couples within each State, though they may vary, subject to constitutional guarantees, from one State to the next. Despite these considerations, it is unnecessary to decide whether this federal intrusion on state power is a violation of the Constitution because it disrupts the federal balance.

The State's power in defining the marital relation is of central relevance in this case quite apart from principles of federalism. Here the State's decision to give this class of persons the right to marry conferred upon them a dignity and status of immense import. When the State used its historic and essential authority to define the marital relation in this way, its role and its power in making the decision enhanced the recognition, dignity, and protection of the class in their own community. DOMA, because of its reach and extent, departs from this history and tradition of reliance on state law to define marriage. "'[D]iscriminations of an unusual character especially suggest careful consideration to determine whether they are obnoxious to the constitutional provision.'" *Romer v. Evans*, 517 U.S. 620 (1996).

The Federal Government uses this state-defined class for the opposite purpose—"to impose restrictions and disabilities." That result requires this Court now to address whether the resulting injury and indignity is a deprivation of an essential part of the liberty protected by the Fifth Amendment. What the State of New York treats as alike the federal law deems unlike by a law designed to injure the same class the State seeks to protect.

In acting first to recognize and then to allow same-sex marriages, New York was responding "to the initiative of those who [sought] a voice in shaping the destiny of their own times." These actions were without doubt a proper exercise of its sovereign authority within our federal system, all in the way that the Framers of the Constitution intended. The dynamics of state government in the federal system are to allow the formation of consensus respecting the way the members of a discrete community treat each other in their daily contact and constant interaction with each other.

The States' interest in defining and regulating the marital relation, subject to constitutional guarantees, stems from the understanding that marriage is more than a routine classification for purposes of certain statutory benefits. Private, consensual sexual intimacy between two adult persons of the same sex may not be punished by the State, and it can form "but one element in a personal bond that is more enduring." *Lawrence v. Texas*, 539 U.S. 558 (2003). By its recognition of the validity of same-sex marriages performed in other jurisdictions and then by authorizing same-sex unions and same-sex marriages, New York sought to give further protection and dignity to that bond. For same-sex couples who wished to be married, the State acted to give their lawful conduct a lawful status. This status is a far-reaching legal acknowledgment of the intimate relationship between two people, a relationship deemed by the State worthy of dignity in the community equal with all other marriages. It reflects both the community's considered perspective on the historical roots of the institution of marriage and its evolving understanding of the meaning of equality.

DOMA seeks to injure the very class New York seeks to protect. By doing so it violates basic due process and equal protection principles applicable to the Federal Government. See U.S. Const., Amdt. 5; *Bolling v. Sharpe*, 347 U.S. 497 (1954). The Constitution's guarantee of equality "must at the very least mean that a bare congressional desire to harm a politically unpopular group cannot" justify disparate treatment of that group. In determining whether a law is motivated by an improper animus or purpose, "'[d]iscriminations of an unusual character'" especially require careful consideration. DOMA cannot survive under these principles. The responsibility of the States for the regulation of domestic relations is an important indicator of the substantial societal impact the State's classifications have in the daily lives and customs of its people. DOMA's unusual deviation from the usual tradition of recognizing and accepting state definitions of marriage here operates to deprive same-sex couples of the benefits and responsibilities that come with the federal recognition of their marriages. This is strong evidence of a law having the purpose and effect of disapproval of that class. The avowed purpose and practical effect of the law here in question are to impose a disadvantage, a separate status, and so a stigma upon all who enter into same-sex marriages made lawful by the unquestioned authority of the States.

The history of DOMA's enactment and its own text demonstrate that interference with the equal dignity of same-sex marriages, a dignity conferred by the States in the exercise of their sovereign power, was more than an incidental effect of the federal statute. It was its essence. The House Report announced its conclusion that "it is both appropriate and necessary for Congress to do what it can to defend the institution of traditional heterosexual marriage. . . . H. R. 3396 is appropriately entitled the 'Defense of Marriage Act.' The effort to redefine 'marriage' to extend to homosexual couples is a truly radical proposal that would fundamentally alter the institution of marriage." The House concluded that DOMA expresses "both moral disapproval of homosexuality, and a moral conviction that heterosexuality better comports with traditional (especially Judeo-Christian) morality." The stated purpose of the law was to promote an "interest in protecting the traditional moral teachings reflected in heterosexual-only marriage laws." Were there any doubt of this far-reaching purpose, the title of the Act confirms it: The Defense of Marriage. . . .

When New York adopted a law to permit same-sex marriage, it sought to eliminate inequality; but DOMA frustrates that objective through a system-wide enactment with no identified connection to any particular area of federal law. DOMA writes inequality into the entire United States Code. The particular case at hand concerns the estate tax, but DOMA is more than a simple determination of what should or should not be allowed as an estate tax refund. Among the over 1,000 statutes and numerous federal regulations that DOMA controls are laws pertaining to Social Security, housing, taxes, criminal sanctions, copyright, and veterans' benefits.

DOMA's principal effect is to identify a subset of state-sanctioned marriages and make them unequal. The principal purpose is to impose inequality, not for other reasons like governmental efficiency. Responsibilities, as well as rights, enhance the dignity and integrity of the person. And DOMA contrives to deprive some couples married under the laws of their State, but not other couples, of both rights and responsibilities. By creating two contradictory marriage regimes within the same State, DOMA forces same-sex couples to live as married for the purpose of state law but unmarried for the purpose of federal law, thus diminishing the stability and predictability of basic personal relations the State has found it proper to acknowledge and protect. By this dynamic DOMA undermines both the public and private significance of state-sanctioned same-sex marriages; for it tells those couples, and all the world, that their otherwise valid marriages are unworthy of federal recognition. This places same-sex couples in an unstable position of being in a second-tier marriage. The differentiation demeans the couple, whose moral and sexual choices the Constitution protects, see *Lawrence*, and whose relationship the State has sought to dignify. And it humiliates tens of thousands of children now being raised by same-sex couples. The law in question makes it even more difficult for the children to understand the integrity and closeness of their own family and its concord with other families in their community and in their daily lives.

Under DOMA, same-sex married couples have their lives burdened, by reason of government decree, in visible and public ways. By its great reach, DOMA touches many aspects of married and family life, from the mundane to the profound. It prevents same-sex married couples from obtaining government healthcare benefits they would otherwise receive. It deprives them of the Bankruptcy Code's special protections for domestic-support obligations. It forces them to follow a complicated procedure to file their state and federal taxes jointly. It prohibits them from being buried together in veterans' cemeteries.

For certain married couples, DOMA's unequal effects are even more serious. The federal penal code makes it a crime to "assaul[t], kidna[p], or murde[r] . . . a member of the immediate family" of "United States official, a United States judge, [or] a Federal law enforcement officer," with the intent to influence or retaliate against that official. Although a "spouse" qualifies as a member of the officer's "immediate family," DOMA makes this protection inapplicable to same-sex spouses. DOMA also brings financial harm to children of same-sex couples. It raises the cost of health care for families by taxing health benefits provided by employers to their workers' same-sex spouses. And it denies or reduces benefits allowed to families upon the loss of a spouse and parent, benefits that are an integral part of family security. DOMA divests married same-sex couples of the duties and responsibilities that are an essential part of married life and that they in most cases would be honored to accept were DOMA not in force. For instance, because it is expected that spouses will support each other as they pursue educational opportunities, federal law takes into consideration a spouse's income in calculating a student's federal financial aid eligibility. Same-sex married couples are exempt from this requirement. The same is true with respect to federal ethics rules. Federal executive and agency officials are prohibited from "participat[ing] personally and substantially" in matters as to which they or their spouses have a financial interest. A similar statute prohibits Senators, Senate employees, and their spouses from accepting high-value gifts from certain sources, and another mandates detailed financial disclosures by numerous high-ranking officials and their spouses. Under DOMA, however, these Government-integrity rules do not apply to same-sex spouses.

The power the Constitution grants it also restrains. And though Congress has great authority to design laws to fit its own conception of sound national policy, it cannot deny the liberty protected by the Due Process Clause of the Fifth Amendment. What has been explained to this point should more than suffice to establish that the principal purpose and the necessary effect of this law are to demean those persons who are in a lawful same-sex marriage. This requires the Court to hold, as it now does, that DOMA is unconstitutional as a deprivation of the liberty of the person protected by the Fifth Amendment of the Constitution.

The liberty protected by the Fifth Amendment's Due Process Clause contains within it the prohibition against denying to any person the equal protection of the laws. While the Fifth Amendment itself withdraws from Government the power to degrade or demean in the way this law does, the equal protection guarantee of the Fourteenth Amendment makes that Fifth Amendment right all the more specific and all the better understood and preserved.

The class to which DOMA directs its restrictions and restraints are those persons who are joined in same-sex marriages made lawful by the State. DOMA singles out a class of persons deemed by a State entitled to recognition and protection to enhance their own liberty. It imposes a disability on the class by refusing to acknowledge a status the State finds to be dignified and proper. DOMA instructs all federal officials, and indeed all persons with whom same-sex couples interact, including their own children, that their marriage is less worthy than the marriages of others. The federal statute is invalid, for no legitimate purpose overcomes the purpose and effect to disparage and to injure those whom the State, by its marriage laws, sought to protect in personhood and dignity. By seeking to displace this protection and treating those persons as living in marriages less respected than others, the federal statute is in violation of the Fifth Amendment. This opinion and its holding are confined to those lawful marriages.

The judgment of the Court of Appeals for the Second Circuit is affirmed.

☐ *CHIEF JUSTICE ROBERTS dissenting.*

I agree with Justice SCALIA that this Court lacks jurisdiction to review the decisions of the courts below. On the merits of the constitutional dispute the Court decides to decide, I also agree with Justice SCALIA that Congress acted constitutionally in passing the Defense of Marriage Act (DOMA). Interests in uniformity and stability amply justified Congress's decision to retain the definition of marriage that, at that point, had been adopted by every State in our Nation, and every nation in the world.

The majority sees a more sinister motive, pointing out that the Federal Government has generally (though not uniformly) deferred to state definitions of marriage in the past. That is true, of course, but none of those prior state-by-state variations had involved differences over something—as the majority puts it—"thought of by most people as essential to the very definition of [marriage] and to its role and function throughout the history of civilization." That the Federal Government treated this fundamental question differently than it treated variations over consanguinity or minimum age is hardly surprising—and hardly enough to support a conclusion that the "principal purpose" of the 342 Representatives and 85 Senators who voted for it, and the President who signed it, was a bare desire to harm.

Nor do the snippets of legislative history and the banal title of the Act to which the majority points suffice to make such a showing. At least without some more convincing evidence that the Act's principal purpose was to codify malice, and that it furthered no legitimate government interests, I would not tar the political branches with the brush of bigotry. . . .

We may in the future have to resolve challenges to state marriage definitions affecting same-sex couples. That issue, however, is not before us in this case, and we hold today that we lack jurisdiction to consider it in the particular context of *Hollingsworth v. Perry*. I write only to highlight the limits of the majority's holding and reasoning today, lest its opinion be taken to resolve not only a question that I believe is not properly before us—DOMA's Constitutionality— but also a question that all agree, and the Court explicitly acknowledges, is not at issue.

☐ *Justice SCALIA, with whom Justice THOMAS joins, and with whom THE CHIEF JUSTICE joins as to Part I, dissenting.*

This case is about power in several respects. It is about the power of our people to govern themselves, and the power of this Court to pronounce the law. Today's opinion aggrandizes the latter, with the predictable consequence of diminishing the former. We have no power to decide this case. And even if we did, we have no power under the Constitution to invalidate this democratically adopted legislation. The Court's errors on both points spring forth from the same diseased root: an exalted conception of the role of this institution in America.

The Court is eager—hungry—to tell everyone its view of the legal question at the heart of this case. Standing in the way is an obstacle, a technicality of little interest to anyone but the people of We the People, who created it as a barrier against judges' intrusion into their lives. They gave judges, in Article III, only the "judicial Power," a power to decide not abstract questions but real, concrete "Cases" and "Controversies." Yet the plaintiff and the Government agree entirely on what should happen in this lawsuit. They agree that the court below got it right; and they agreed in the court below that the court below that one got it right as well. What, then, are we doing here?

The answer lies at the heart of the jurisdictional portion of today's opinion, where a single sentence lays bare the majority's vision of our role. The Court says that we have the power to decide this case because if we did not, then our "primary role in determining the constitutionality of a law" (at least one that "has inflicted real injury on a plaintiff") would "become only secondary to the President's." But wait, the reader wonders—Windsor won below, and so cured her injury, and the President was glad to see it. True, says the majority, but judicial review must march on regardless, lest we "undermine the clear dictate of the separation-of-powers principle that when an Act of Congress is alleged to conflict with the Constitution, it is emphatically the province and duty of the judicial department to say what the law is."

That is jaw-dropping. It is an assertion of judicial supremacy over the people's Representatives in Congress and the Executive. It envisions a Supreme Court standing (or rather enthroned) at the apex of government, empowered to decide all constitutional questions, always and everywhere "primary" in its role. This image of the Court would have been unrecognizable to those who wrote and ratified our national charter. They knew well the dangers of "primary" power, and so created branches of government that would be "perfectly coordinate by the terms of their common commission," none of which branches could "pretend to an exclusive or superior right of settling the boundaries between their respective powers." *The Federalist*, No. 49. The people did this to protect themselves. They did it to guard their right to self-rule against the black-robed supremacy that today's majority finds so attractive. So it was that Madison could confidently state, with no fear of contradiction, that there was nothing of "greater intrinsic value" or "stamped with the authority of more enlightened patrons of liberty" than a government of separate and coordinate powers.

For this reason we are quite forbidden to say what the law is whenever (as today's opinion asserts) "'an Act of Congress is alleged to conflict with the Constitution.'" We can do so only when that allegation will determine the outcome of a lawsuit, and is contradicted by the other party. The "judicial Power" is not, as the majority believes, the power "'to say what the law is,'" giving the Supreme Court the "primary role in determining the constitutionality of laws." The majority must have in mind one of the foreign constitutions that pronounces such primacy for its constitutional court and allows that primacy to be exercised in contexts other than a lawsuit. The judicial power as Americans have understood it (and their English ancestors before them) is the power to adjudicate, with conclusive effect, disputed government claims (civil or criminal) against private persons, and disputed claims by private persons against the government or other private persons. Sometimes (though not always) the parties before the court disagree not with regard to the facts of their case (or not only with regard to the facts) but with regard to the applicable law "in which event (and only in which event) it becomes the 'province and duty of the judicial department to say what the law is.'"

In other words, declaring the compatibility of state or federal laws with the Constitution is not only not the "primary role" of this Court, it is not a separate, free-standing role at all. We perform that role incidentally—by accident, as it were—when that is necessary to resolve the dispute before us. Then, and only then, does it become "the province and duty of the judicial department to say what the law is." That is why, in 1793, we politely declined the Washington Administration's request to "say what the law is" on a particular treaty matter that was not the subject of a concrete legal controversy. And that is why, as our opinions have said, some questions of law will never be presented to this Court, because there will never be anyone with standing to bring a lawsuit. . . .

For the reasons above, I think that this Court has, and the Court of Appeals had, no power to decide this suit. We should vacate the decision below and remand to the Court of Appeals for the Second Circuit, with instructions to dismiss the appeal. . . .

☐ *Justice ALITO, with whom Justice THOMAS joins as to Parts II nd III, dissenting.*

Our Nation is engaged in a heated debate about same-sex marriage. That debate is, at bottom, about the nature of the institution of marriage. Respondent Edith Windsor, supported by the United States, asks this Court to intervene in that debate, and although she couches her argument in different terms, what she seeks is a holding that enshrines in the Constitution a particular understanding of marriage under which the sex of the partners makes no difference. The Constitution, however, does not dictate that choice. It leaves the choice to the people, acting through their elected representatives at both the federal and state levels. I would therefore hold that Congress did not violate Windsor's constitutional rights by enacting Section 3 of the Defense of Marriage Act (DOMA), which defines the meaning of marriage under federal statutes that either confer upon married persons certain federal benefits or impose upon them certain federal obligations. . . .

In my view, the United States clearly is not a proper petitioner in this case. The United States does not ask us to overturn the judgment of the court below or to alter that judgment in any way. Quite to the contrary, the United States argues emphatically in favor of the correctness of that judgment. We have never before reviewed a decision at the sole behest of a party that took such a position, and to do so would be to render an advisory opinion, in violation of Article III's dictates. For the reasons given in Justice SCALIA's dissent, I do not find the Court's arguments to the contrary to be persuasive. . . .

INDEX OF CASES

Cases printed in boldface are excerpted on the page(s) printed in boldface.

Agency for International Development v. Alliance for Open Society International, Inc., 56–57

Alleyne v. United States, 110

American Tradition Partnership v. Bullock, 40

American Trucking Associations v. City of Los Angeles, 36

Apprendi v. New Jersey, 110

Arizona Christian School Tuition Organization v. Winn, 8, **9–12**

Arizona Free Enterprise Club's Freedom Club PAC v. Bennett, 39–40, **40–47**

Arizona v. Evans, 96

Arizona v. Gant, 92–96

Arizona v. Inter Tribal Council of Arizona, 36, 40, 48

Arizona v. United States, 35

Arkansas Game and Fish Commission v. United States, 49

Armour v. City of Indianapolis, 117

Ashcroft v. American Civil Liberties Union, 58

AT&T Mobility v. Concepcion, 7, 34

Bailey v. United States, 87

Bell v. Wolfish, 86

Blueford v. Arkansas, 112

Bolling v. Sharpe, 123

Bond v. United States, 9

Bowen v. Kendrick, 11

Boyd v. United States, 82

Brandenburg v. Ohio, 58

Brigham City v. Stuart, 89–90

Brown v. Entertainment Merchants Association, 56, **57–62**

Brown v. Plata, 7, 114

Bruesewitz v. Wyeth, 33

Buckley v. Valeo, 39, 41–47

Bullcoming v. New Mexico, 111

California v. Ciraolo, 82

Camreta v. Greene, 3

Chamber of Commerce v. Whiting, 34

Chaplinsky v. New Hampshire, 58, 61

Chevron v. Natural Resources Defense Council, 15

Chimel v. California, 93

Church of Lukumi Babalu Aye, Inc. v. Hialeah, 59

Citizens United v. Federal Election Commission, 39–43, 47

City of Arlington v. FCC, 15

Clapper v. Amnesty International, 9

Cline v. Oklahoma Coalition for Reproductive Justice, 116

Coleman v. Court of Appeals of Maryland, 36

Colorado Republican Federal Campaign Comm. v. Federal Election Comm'n (Colorado I), 42

Comcast v. Behrend, 14

Crawford v. Washington, 110–111

Dan's City Used Cars v. Pelkey, 35

Davis v. Federal Election Commission, 39, 42–43

Davis v. United States, **92–96**

Dickerson v. United States, 99
District Attorney's Office for Third Judicial
    District v. Osborne, 53–54
Doe v. Reed, 47
Dollan v. City of Tigard, 50
Doremus v. Board of Education of
    Hawthorne, 10
Dun & Bradstreet, Inc. v. Greenmoss
    Builders, Inc., 66

Elkins v. United States, 94
Entick v. Carrington, 73, 82
Eu v. San Francisco County Democratic
    Central Comm., 41
Evans v. Michigan, 113

FCC v. Fox Television Stations, Inc., 54,
    64
FCC v. Pacifica Foundation, 64
Federal Election Commission v. Colorado
    Republican Federal Campaign Comm.,
    (Colorado II), 42
Federal Election Commission v.
    Massachusetts Citizens for Life, 41–42
Fisher v. University of Texas at Austin,
    118
Flast v. Cohen, 4, 8–9, 11–12
Florence v. Board of Chosen Freeholders, 86
Florida v. Harris, 71, 91
Florida v. Jardines, 71, 80–86
Frothingham v. Mellon, 10

Ginsberg v. New York, 57–58
Golan v. Holder, 55
Goldman v. United States, 76
Gonzales v. Raich, 22, 27–28
Griffin v. California, 98, 101–102
Griffith v. Kentucky, 94, 96
Grutter v. Bollinger, 118

Hammer v. Dagenhart, 26
Harris v. United States, 110
Heart of Atlanta Motel, Inc. v. United
    States, 21
Hein v. Freedom from Religion
    Foundation, Inc., 8, 10
Helvering v. Davis, 30
Herring v. United States, 96

Hester v. United States, 82
Hill v. Lockhart, 106–107
Hillman v. Maretta, 35
Hollingsworth v. Perry, 3, 4–7, 119,
    126
Hosanna-Tabor Evangelical Lutheran Church
    and School v. Equal Employment
    Opportunity Commission, 68
Howes v. Fields, 97, 101
Hustler Magazine, Inc. v. Falwell, 66

Illinois v. Caballes, 83, 91
Illinois v. Krull, 96
Illinois v. Lidster, 79

J. D. B. v. North Carolina, 97, 98–101
Joseph Burstyn, Inc. v. Wilson, 58–59

Katzenbach v. McClung, 21
Katz v. United States, 73–77, 79, 81,
    83–85
Kentucky v. King, 87, 88–90
Koontz v. St. Johns River Water
    Management District, 49
Kurns v. Railroad Friction Products
    Corporation, 34
Kyllo v. United States, 73, 83–85

Lafler v. Cooper, 104–107
Lawrence v. Texas, 122, 124
Linkletter v. Walker, 94–96
Lochner v. New York, 63
Loving v. Virginia, 121
Lujan v. Defenders of Wildlife, 5, 10

Mapp v. Ohio, 94, 96
Marbury v. Madison, 19
Maryland v. King, 70, 103
Maryland v. Wirtz, 21
M. B. Z. v. Clinton, 3
McConnell v. Federal Election Commission,
    39, 42
Michigan v. Bryant, 111
Michigan v. Summers, 87
Miller v. Alabama, 115
Miller v. California, 58
Mincey v. Arizona, 89
Miranda v. Arizona, 97–102

Missouri v. Frye, 104–105, **105–110**
Missouri v. McNeely, 87, 102

National Federation of Independent Business v. Sebelius, 17, **18–32**
National Labor Relations Board v. Canning, 16
National Meat Association v. Harris, 34
Nevada Commission on Ethics v. Carrington, 48
Nevada Department of Human Resources v. Hibbs, 36
New York Times Co. v. Sullivan, 44, 66
New York v. Belton, 93–94
New York v. United States, 22–24
Nixon v. Shrink Missouri Government PA, 42
NLRB v. Jones & Laughlin Steel Corp., 26
Nollan v. California Coastal Commission, 50

Oliver v. United States, 74, 81
Olmstead v. United States, 73, 76

Padilla v. Kentucky, 106–107, 109
Payton v. New York, 89
Pennsylvania Bd. of Probation and Parole v. Scott, 94
People v. Defore, 95
Perez v. United States, 19
Perry v. Perez, 37
Planned Parenthood of Southeastern Pennsylvania v. Casey, 116
Pliva, Inc. v. Mensing, 34
Printz v. United States, 24

Regents of the University of California v. Bakke, 118
Romer v. Evans, 122
Roper v. Simmons, 62
Roth v. United States, 58
Rust v. Sullivan, 47, 57

Salinas v. Texas, 98, 101
Schmerber v. California, 87, 102
Schuette v. Coalition to Defend Affirmative Action, 118
Skinner v. Switzer, 54

Snyder v. Phelps, 64, **65–67**
Shelby County, Alabama v. Holder, 38
Silverman v. United States, 76, 82
Sorrell v. IMS Health Inc., 63
Sosna v. Iowa, 121
Sossamon v. Texas, 36
South Dakota v. Dole, 19, 24
Southern Union Company v. United States, 110
Stansbury v. California, 100
State v. Gant, 93
Steward Machine Co. v. Davis, 24
Stone v. Powell, 94
Strickland v. Washington, 106–109

Tennant v. Jefferson County Commission, 38
Thompson v. Keohane, 100
Town of Greece v. Galloway, 69
Turner v. Rogers, 54

United States v. Alvarez, 56
United States v. Darby, 26
United States v. Jacobsen, 83
United States v. Jones, 71, **72–80,** 81, 83
United States v. Karo, 74, 76
United States v. Knotts, 73, 75, 79, 81
United States v. Leon, 94–96
United States v. Lopez, 29, 32
United States v. Morrison, 19, 29
United States v. Place, 83
United States v. Reorganized CF&I Fabricators of Utah, Inc., 23
United States v. Santana, 90
United States v. Stevens, 58
United States v. Windsor, 119, **120–128**

Valley Forge Christian College v. Americans United for Separation of Church and State, Inc., 8

Wal-Mart Stores, Inc. v. Dukes, 7
Weeks v. United States, 94, 96
Wickard v. Filburn, 19–21, 28, 31
Williamson v. Mazda Motor of America, 33
Williams v. Illinois, 111
WOS v. E.M.A., 34

Other Books by David M. O'Brien

Storm Center:
The Supreme Court in American Politics
10th ed.

Constitutional Law and Politics:
Vol. 1. *Struggles for Power and Governmental Accountability*
Vol. 2. *Civil Rights and Civil Liberties*
9th ed.

Congress Shall Make No Law: The First Amendment,
Unprotected Expression, and the U.S. Supreme Court

Animal Sacrifice and Religious Freedom:
Church of Lukumi Babalu Aye v. City of Hialeah

To Dream of Dreams:
Religious Freedom and Constitutional Politics in Postwar Japan

Judicial Roulette

What Process Is Due?
Courts and Science-Policy Disputes

The Public's Right to Know:
The Supreme Court and the First Amendment

Privacy, Law, and Public Policy

Judges on Judging: Views from the Bench
4th ed. (editor)

The Lanahan Readings on Civil Rights and Civil Liberties
3rd ed. (editor)

Abortion and American Politics
(co-author)

Judicial Independence in the Age of Democracy:
Critical Perspectives from Around the World
(co-editor)

The Politics of Technology Assessment:
Institutions, Processes, and Policy Disputes
(co-editor)

Views from the Bench:
The Judiciary and Constitutional Politics
(co-editor)

The Politics of American Government
3rd ed. (co-author)

Government by the People
22nd ed. (co-author)

Courts and Judicial Policymaking
(co-author)